T·h·e
Mommy and Daddy Guide to Kindergarten

*Real-Life Advice and Tips from
Parents and Other Experts*

A to Z

Susan Bernard
with Cary O. Yager

CB
CONTEMPORARY BOOKS

Library of Congress Cataloging-in-Publication Data

Bernard, Susan, 1950–
    The mommy and daddy guide to kindergarten : real-life advice and tips from parents
and other experts / Susan Bernard with Cary O. Yager.
        p.   cm.
    Includes bibliographical references.
    ISBN 0-8092-2547-6
    1. Kindergarten—United States.   2. Kindergarten—Parent participation—United States.
3. Interviews—United States.   I. Yager, Cary O.   II. Title.
LB1195 .B37   2000
372.21'8—dc21   00-31411
                                                      CIP

To my dear husband and best friend, Bernie Rotondo, for his unwavering belief in and support of all my endeavors, and to our son, Alex Bernard Rotondo, my source of inspiration and greatest joy!

In memory of my father, Berny Schwartz (1920–1989), and with love to my mother, Marjorie L. Schwartz.

Susan Bernard

To Ken, my compass, and our beautiful boys, Oley and CJ, for the wonder and magic they bring to my life. And to Linda, Patsy, Jim, and Roy (we miss you, Pop!) for their patience, guidance, and wisdom.

Cary O. Yager

Cover design by Jeanette Wojtyla
Cover illustrations by Laura Jane Coats
Interior design by Susan H. Hartman

Published by Contemporary Books
A division of NTC/Contemporary Publishing Group, Inc.
4255 West Touhy Avenue, Lincolnwood (Chicago), Illinois 60712-1975 U.S.A.
Printed in the United States of America
International Standard Book Number: 0-8092-2547-6

01 02 03 04 05 06 QM 18 17 16 15 14 13 12 11 10 9 8 7 6 5 4 3 2 1

Contents

Acknowledgments

I thank the following people for their support, friendship, and professional expertise:

Cary O. Yager, whose skills in interviewing and editing are surpassed only by her sense of humor;

Brenda Koplin, "my" copyeditor par excellence, who continues to watch over my grammar, provide support, tolerate procrastination, and laugh at my essays;

Susan Moore-Kruse, editorial team leader for NTC/Contemporary Publishing Group, who has so skillfully shepherded my book through the editorial process, and though I have missed every conceivable deadline, has shown great kindness and patience;

Susan H. Hartman, who created a terrific interior book design; Alison Shurtz, NTC/Contemporary's copyeditor, who did such a conscientious and thorough job; Judith N. McCarthy, NTC/Contemporary's senior editor, who has enthusiastically supported this project;

As always, Nancy Crossman, my agent, who steadfastly believes in my work, calmly handles my seismic mood swings from elation to dismay, and ardently represents my books;

Barbara Wong, a dear friend with enormous expertise as a kindergarten teacher and principal, who provided inestimable support and answered all my questions;

Sherry Kaufman and Sandra Chon Wang, model kindergarten teachers, who provided important information and funny anecdotes;

Michelle Bennett, principal extraordinaire at Westwood Charter Elementary School, for her insight and wisdom;

Arlene Garbus, who so seamlessly integrates curriculum and who taught my son, Alex, how fun and challenging learning can be, appreciated his strengths, allowed his creativity to flourish, and instilled in him a lifelong intellectual confidence;

Sue Polep, another champion of creativity, who taught my son and his classmates how to organize class projects, meet deadlines, and make polished presentations, thus making the transition to middle school a breeze;

Pam Dresher, Steven Siegel, Sally Roten, Scott Kubota, Lili Flanders, and the score of other parents who shared their stories, and to the children of Westwood Charter Elementary School who allowed me to see firsthand what kindergarten is all about;

Linda Spector, Peter Jacobson, Jeffrey Duclos, Gretchen Thompson, Susan Dutton, Rita Lowenthal, Anne Farrell, Linda Castile, Claudia Hudgens, Bill and Tricia Flumenbaum, and Dr. Michael Rosenblatt for their friendship, help, and support;

My sister, Jane Schwartz-Jaffe, who helped with the parents' quotes, and Gib, Samantha, and Nick Jaffe;

Jim and Anneliese Schwartz; Tracy, Jon, and Julia Hughes; Zachary Schwartz; Marilyn and Sandy Bauman; Teresa Rotondo; Sandra Zarember; and Cami and Dave Black, my extended family; and

Lillian Katz, Ph.D., and her marvelous ERIC®, the Educational Resources Information Center Clearinghouse on Elementary and Early Childhood Education, and Barbara Warman at the National Association for the Education of Young Children.

Finally, thanks to all the subject matter experts whose contributions are invaluable and without whom this book could not have been written.

Introduction

It has been more than six years since our son, Alex, began kindergarten, although I feel like it was yesterday. While my husband, Bernie, and I knew Alex would be attending an excellent neighborhood school, still, I had a slew of questions. And although Bernie remained calm and silent, I was sure he did too.

From the moment we enrolled Alex, I began obsessing. What would his first day be like? Would he feel like I was flinging him out of preschool without a safety net? Would he suffer from separation anxiety? Would he like his new teacher? Would the curriculum be interesting? Would he make new friends easily? Would he feel safe? How would a child who marches to the beat of a different drummer adapt to a structured environment?

Since I was working three full days a week and kindergarten was a little more than three hours a day, would the after-school program work out? Should I work less? Would the adjustment of Alex starting kindergarten with new children and attending a new after-school program with kindergartners from different classrooms be overwhelming?

Bernie and I and our friends and their spouses grappled with these issues and more. We had philosophical discussions about the purpose of kindergarten. What were our kids supposed to learn and how well had we prepared them? If we (or their preschool teachers) had taught them too much, would they be bored? If we hadn't taught them enough, would they lag behind? Or perhaps academics were not as important as socialization. Come time for report cards, would our children's teachers care more about whether they'd memorized the letters of the alphabet, made friends, or behaved with civility in the classroom? Independent of how our kids were assessed, what would their first-grade teachers expect them to know?

Despite our doubts and concerns, Alex, Bernie, and I survived kindergarten. During the intervening years, as I watched Alex and his friends progress through elementary school, I continued thinking about the kindergarten year. I noticed that some of his classmates who had problems then—whether academic, social, or behavioral—still had them. The ones who'd improved had usually benefited from some sort of intervention, whether it was in the form of individual instruction, speech therapy, pull-out classes, or counseling. Many of the kids who thrived early on, continued to do so, although there were certainly exceptions.

My growing interest in the impact of kindergarten fueled my passion to begin researching *The Mommy and Daddy Guide to Kindergarten: Real-Life Advice and Tips from Parents and Other Experts*. For this book, I teamed up with Cary O. Yager (whose sons Oley and Carter will be attending kindergarten soon), and together we interviewed some seventy experts, including educators, psychologists, and researchers in reading, writing, mathematics, science, and social studies. We talked with authorities in the fields of art and music, computing, motor development, and assessment (testing and report cards) and others who specialize in age-appropriate behavior, home-schooling, kindergarten readiness, preschool preparation, gifted children, special needs children, and a host of other interesting topics. Some of the people we interviewed are well-known personalities. There are others whose names you may not recognize but who are the best and the brightest in their fields.

They shared their insight, wisdom, and advice. I silently laughed as they so easily resolved problems that had seemed so overwhelming to me and my friends just a few years earlier. I kept saying to myself, over and over and over, "If I had only known then what I know now. . . ."

I interviewed other experts: kindergarten teachers throughout the country, who most directly influence our children's lives as they begin their formal educational experience. They teach in a variety of elementary schools throughout the country—from Central Kindergarten, with 700 kindergarten children, in Eden Prairie, Minnesota, to Westwood Charter Elementary School, with 120 kindergarten children, in Los Angeles, California, to Harborview Elementary School, with 30 kindergartners, in Juneau, Alaska.

What I learned is that good teachers, no matter where they teach and live, share similar qualities. They're nurturing and supportive, creative and enthusiastic. They delight in our children's successes and challenges. They help them, and us, deal with our issues—be they separation anxiety, age-appropriate behavior, or homework headaches. They reach out to our children and to us, knowing that parental involvement makes all the difference in whether children learn and enjoy school or feel that school must not be important because no one in their family gets involved and shows they care.

There are teachers who so seamlessly integrate their curriculum that when our children learn social studies, they are also learning music and dance. Reading, writing, and language arts go hand in hand. Learning math and science is stimulating, even joyful. (Can that really be?) Playing not only is fun, but as Dr. Jerome Singer from Yale University says, "It becomes the foundation for the inner resources of imagination that every adult requires."

We learn that those things our children do that sometimes concern us may simply be considered age-appropriate behavior. As Jacqueline Haines from the Gessell Institute of Human Development says, kindergarten is a time of "dramatic change." If a child is five, he or she may be "compliant and cooperative with a sunny disposition." But as children turn six, they are more likely to engage in power struggles. "They know everything and can do everything."

Of course, if we are honest, we might acknowledge that sometimes we, too, feel as if we know everything. But there are moments of insecurity and self-doubt—feelings I unabashedly share in my essays, whether they are my own stories or those of others. (I've set up the book so that every chapter features one of my essays followed by interviews with, or material provided by, our experts. Some chapters also include position papers from national organizations.)

For those of us whose children have moved on from kindergarten, or are currently in kindergarten, we look back and laugh at how uptight and tense we were. For those of us whose children soon will be kindergartners, we may already be feeling that lump in our throats that our friends assure us will eventually dissolve once our children start first grade.

And nowadays, there is additional anxiety and some controversy as well. As standardized testing has become the be-all and end-all for measuring success, we suddenly find that our kids are stressed out and we are too. Some of us wonder why a kindergarten child needs to learn to read. My son, Alex, didn't learn until the second grade, and he started out reading at a fourth-grade level. In moments of reflection we ask ourselves, must kindergarten children learn to count to forty when some of them started school without counting at all, and others don't choose to count even if they know how?

Is all this pressure making us lose our collective judgment as we enroll our five-year-old children in "mini-SAT" courses so that they can learn to read and write before their peers? And what effect is this having on our children? To paraphrase Dr. Samuel Meisels, a testing authority from the University of Michigan, "All of a sudden, our children realize there are consequences for doing poorly, that it's not okay to ask questions, and that their teacher is not there to help them."

We wonder if it's necessary to foist this new neurosis, kindergarten angst, upon our children. Or is there another way to look at it? For some of us, kindergarten is also a wondrous time. It's the period when we see our "babies" (even if they are five or six years old) gain independence. There is an indescribable feeling of joy when they walk out of elementary school with huge smiles on their faces, and their first journal tucked under their arm. We want to cry when they greet us with a frown because a friend was "mean" or they had an "accident" (although they haven't had one in years).

As parents whose child is just starting middle school, but who have nieces, nephews, and friends with children who will begin kindergarten, Bernie and I remember that kindergarten year with Alex as one of our most emotional yet exciting ones.

With all the pressure we and others are now putting on ourselves and our children—whether it's to test better or learn faster—I sometimes feel we must remember the genesis of kindergarten. When Friedrich Froebel, a nineteenth-century German educator who is considered the father of kindergarten, conceived the idea, he literally pictured it as a "garden of children." It was a time for them to grow, mature, and blossom.

As we push our children through the kindergarten of the twenty-first century, we might take the time to rethink this original premise. Should kindergarten be a time of stress and pressure, for them and for us? Or should we give childhood back to our children?

Once again, Bernie thinks I'm being melodramatic. "Okay, so let the kids sit in a garden," he said. "But in case they want more intellectual stimulation, would it hurt to give them a few books, some marbles to play with or to count, and some paper to write or draw on?"

As I shook my head and laughed, I realized that there is a reason why I'm married to Bernie and also why I named this book *The Mommy and Daddy Guide to Kindergarten*. After all, everything is a matter of perspective, and sometimes our husbands are even right!

Age-Appropriate Behavior

After a few weeks of kindergarten, once mothers began volunteering in the classrooms, I was somewhat amazed by the developmental differences among Alex's peers. Compared to his preschool playmates—a somewhat homogeneous group—this class was composed of thirty-two kids with different backgrounds, lifestyles, abilities, sensibilities, and behavioral patterns.

We liked the mix, which was why we sent Alex to public school. But it suddenly seemed as if we were pushing our child out of a cloistered preschool nest into a volatile kindergarten cauldron.

As a weekly classroom volunteer, I was quite surprised by the wide range of children's behavior. A thin, gangly kid named Benjamin evidently was competing for the *Guinness Book of World Records* for rule breaking. It was perfectly clear to me that pushing, grabbing, and finger painting other children was not age-appropriate behavior, but I wondered whether a lack of listening, nose picking, and brashness was.

Then there was Hailey, a cute little girl whose level of separation anxiety defied anything I'd ever seen or read about.

Compared to my daughter, Hannah, some of the other kids' behavior seemed so immature. When I found out they were four years and nine months old, I knew why.

Debby, mother of Tyler, 3, and Hannah, 6

For the first two months of school, she cried every single morning when her parents said good-bye. Could this behavior be considered an endearing, albeit dramatic expression of parental love, or was it just pure kindergarten angst?

After many weeks of observance, I suspected that nail biting, thumb sucking, pencil chewing, and throat clearing were well within the normal range. And I was quite sure that kicking down one's playmate's blocks, affixing paste to her hair, grabbing his snacks, and spitting at one another were not.

I wonder what would happen if adults' behavior was classified as age appropriate.

Brian, father of
Tommy, 5

But there were some questionable areas, as well. Although I knew that parent volunteers were expected to adhere to a strict policy of confidentiality regarding classroom behavior, I finally couldn't remain silent for one more minute. I called another mom who has an advanced degree in educational psychology and explained my quandary. She told me that some rules are made to be broken—that gossiping, as a means of information exchange, is not a sin—and asked what was bothering me.

"I guess it all revolves around what is 'normal' behavior for a kindergarten child," I said. "Is it age appropriate for Jack not only to tear up Sylvie's picture but also to laugh when he does it, for Jessica to deny all behavioral indiscretions—she seems to lie all the time—and Morgan to surreptitiously place boogers on anyone who's sitting in front of him? And what about Alden wetting his pants, Ramie throwing sand, and Caitlin refusing to eat any food during snack or lunch time?"

Ellen laughed aloud. "First, you need to know that there is a large spectrum of behavior that is considered 'normal'— or perhaps 'usual' is a better word. What I'd suggest is that you read the Gesell Institute's *Your Five-Year-Old: Sunny and Serene.* After years of research, they've really nailed down behavioral patterns."

"Five is sunny and serene? You've got to be kidding."

"Not really," she thoughtfully answered. "Just look at Alex. At five, most kids truly want to be good, and in fact, are. What you're dealing with in kindergarten are children whose ages may range by one full year, and whose maturity span is even wider."

We talked further, and I felt much better before I hung up. Later that week, when Alex had a play date and his new friend peed on my azaleas, it didn't phase me.

What to Expect from Kindergartners

Jacqueline Haines is the executive director of the Gessell Institute of Human Development. Louise Bates Ames, Ph.D., cofounder of the institute, and the late Frances L. Ilg, M.D., are the authors of a series of books that includes *Your One-Year-Old* through *Your Ten- to Fourteen-Year-Old*.

What are the characteristics of a "normal" five-year-old and six-year-old?

All kindergartners go through pretty dramatic changes. The five-year-old is compliant, cooperative, and interested in how letters and numbers work. Five wants to be good, works to be good, and more often than not, succeeds in being good. Perhaps most delightful of all his characteristics is that he enjoys life so much and looks so consistently on its sunny side.

Six-year-olds are more into power struggles. They know everything. They can do everything, and they have a terrible time taking responsibility for any misbehavior. It is always someone else's fault. Six-year-olds are aware of what is going on in their world. Five-year-olds have not sorted out how everything works, so there is a great deal of self-protection.

Six-year-olds are bossy, to the point that sometimes there is a conflict with their teacher and their parents. They think both teachers and parents should do whatever they want them to. They get into power struggles with adults and with other children. Parents have to diffuse the situation by saying things like, "I'm sorry. I didn't see what happened. I hope you remember the rule next time."

Are there differences between boys and girls?

The boys seem to take a little bit longer to settle down. They are certainly not as interested in the paper-and-pencil tasks as the girls are. They much prefer hands-on activities. In general, boys have a very different way of solving problems than girls do. Girls use language and written symbols much more readily than boys do. Boys are often more creative in their problem solving. They like materials like blocks and action figures. It doesn't mean that they don't use good language, they just like to look at things from various angles. Little girls like to produce their ideas as quickly as they can and are more likely to talk their problems through.

What is considered "age-appropriate behavior" in kindergarten?

Even if children have attended preschool, at first they are anxious. They are not sure what school is all about. Some children will begin to stutter or stammer when they are trying to get their ideas across. They are very tied into the teacher and want to be accepted by her.

Kindergartners are cooperative and rule oriented. They do things a certain way and set up their own rules in the play corner or wherever they are. They adore imitating adults in pretend play and putting their ideas down either in creative art form or in block play. They are involved in pretend play. At this age their pretend play has reality to it, whereas at preschool age it does not. Girls and boys let each other play in their activities, but that will disappear soon.

Kindergartners' behavior is not as calm at the end of the year as it was at the beginning of the year. As the children turn older they become very emotional. They begin to go through what we call the breakup stage. Because of rapid brain growth they begin to experience some confusion

What does the term "age-appropriate" behavior mean? Is it a euphemism for being poorly behaved?

Marc, father of Sam, 7

about how things work. They will have an idea and then try out a solution. If it doesn't work, they become frustrated. They also become resistant to change. So in general during the kindergarten year, the teacher will do well if he or she has clear routines and rituals.

Do children usually go through a physical growth spurt in kindergarten?

Yes. Five-year-olds are losing their baby roundness and getting taller, and a little more leggy. Six-year-olds are experiencing quick growth. That is why they are so awkward. They are not neat in their writing. In fact, they are messy. They don't do well with their cutting skills.

What do you think of the academic emphasis in kindergarten?

There is now a strong level of anxiety in our culture that our children are not going to live up to someone's expectations. I don't know whose. There is wonderful research on the whole business of teaching things too soon. Concepts that are taught before children are neurologically ready for them can create real problems later on. They create a lot of gaps in learning. Children get only bits and pieces of information. Then they have to catch up and put these bits and pieces together as they move on to higher-level thinking. Because of this disparity, many educators are backing off a bit and doing a lot more concept exploring rather than just pushing more and more and more information on children.

It is much healthier to build a solid foundation. It is better for children to feel they are well grounded, and know what they know. The need to complete tasks and feel closure before moving on is extremely important. Some of the behavioral issues that teachers talk about is the frustration that comes from a lack of closure.

It is also important to realize that more is not always better. Some children have a built-in temperament of intensity and drive. They love doing more and that is fine. But those

My younger daughter, Libby, was one of the youngest in her class. She didn't listen; she squirmed during circle time. After the fifth time in three weeks that her teacher told me her behavior was disruptive, I burst into tears. Suddenly the teacher became more sympathetic, so I'd recommend crying if things aren't working out.

Melinda, mother of Libby, 8, Shawn, 10, and Royce, 15

qualities should not be imposed on others. If one child likes doing twelve pages per day in a workbook, and another likes completing one, both are okay. Some schools understand what youngsters can handle, on a cognitive basis, from age to age. They apply this as their baseline and then add a lot of enrichment. Those children fare much better later on. There needs to be flexibility in what is offered. One system does not fit all.

Art

I asked Shay, an acquaintance and former teacher now a painter, how well she thought art was taught in kindergarten.

"In many schools, art is taught better in kindergarten than in any other grade," she said. "In the best programs, it is thoroughly integrated into the curriculum. Children use art to learn reading, writing, arithmetic, social science, and social studies.

"The art budget is usually better in kindergarten. There are a lot of available materials, including crayons, tempera paints, watercolors, finger paints, clay, and play dough. Children color, draw, cut, paste, model, make collages, and use papier-mâché.

"A good teacher will talk with her students about colors and how to mix them, and will explain texture, line, and design. She will encourage creativity and exploration. She will not focus on pretty finished products that parents will coo over but that the children are usually unable to complete on their own."

"So you're saying that kindergarten art programs are good."

"Some are," she answered. "In many cases, teachers are doing a good job teaching the visual arts. Still, most programs

Rory has always shown a talent for art. My two favorite kindergarten projects that he made were an orange walnut necklace for Halloween and a little wooden box with different shaped macaroni and multicolored beans glued on top. He handled it better than I did when his younger sister tried to feed our dog the macaroni and beans. Luckily the glue was strongly affixed.

Stephanie, mother
of Lucy, 2, and
Rory, 6

could be better. In the best programs children learn how to look at art. They are taken to museums to see what different types of art look like. They begin learning to distinguish styles of painting. They start exploring the richness of color and how different painters apply it to their work. They develop a familiarity with names like Bearden, Cassatt, Kahlo, Renoir, Rothenberg, Rivera, Van Gogh."

"Do you think the children's parents can identify these artists?" I asked. "I wonder how many people are interested in art history these days."

She shook her head and shrugged.

"And you really think kindergartners can grasp this?"

"Why not? At any early age, exposure is critical. The children will understand what they are able to and will build their knowledge base each year."

"You won't get an argument from me," I responded. "But what is the art budget?"

"Not as much as it should be, but it's growing."

"I didn't realize you were such an advocate for the arts."

"It was unavoidable," Shay replied. "I've got three kids in school."

"Yeah, I understand." After looking at my watch I abruptly said, "Listen, I've got an important phone call. We'll talk soon."

We said good-bye. I got into my car, drove a few blocks away, picked up my cellular phone, and when the information operator asked, "What number do you want?" I answered, "The Los Angeles County Museum of Art."

I guess it's never too late to help your child develop more cultural sensibilities.

I've blocked out what Sara made, but I'll never forget how difficult it was to scrub and wash the glue, paint, glitter, and who knows what else from her jeans. Finally, I stopped trying, although I felt somewhat guilty when she went to school looking like a ragamuffin.

Alisa, mother of
Sara, 6, and Eli, 10

Celebrating Art

Jessica Davis, Ed.D., is the Patricia Bauman Chair in Arts in Education, Harvard University Graduate School of Education.

What role does art play in kindergarten?

All kindergartners come to school with the gifts of artistry: drawing pictures, singing songs, getting deeply involved in pretend play and, unfortunately, too often they leave school without any attachment to those activities. But in kindergarten, fortunately for children age five—the golden age of creativity—teachers seem excited about these gifts and eager to give children the chance to exercise them.

What constitutes a good program in the arts?

A good art curriculum at the kindergarten level acknowledges and celebrates the gifts that preschool children bring to school and works to develop those gifts as important forms of expression in themselves, not just as means to move on to reading, writing, and arithmetic. A good program recognizes that the arts express things that can't be expressed in other disciplines. Too often the arts are used at the kindergarten level as transitional activities to set children up for something else. The drawing is enjoyed only as a step toward writing. Pretend play is necessary this year only because soon children have those roles down and we can move on to talking about them in another way.

The arts are used to set the stage for more traditional learning skills. And that's too bad. It's too bad that a five-year-old's drawing will be written on. For example, a teacher will write *mommy*, *daddy*, *brother*, *sister* right on the drawing, suggesting that the picture doesn't say enough. The message sent to the child is "Once I can write those words, I won't need to draw anymore." So much is lost when we let children give up those wonderful early skills rather than acknowledging that they are unique, very capable people who know how to make these wonderful things that we prize and cherish.

With cutbacks, is art still being taught in most elementary schools?

It's very hard to know what's going on where. There seem to be many more arts magnet schools and pilot schools

Danielle's teacher was into "pretty" things. The problem was that none of the children could make them to her satisfaction, so she "fixed" them all. The parents were afraid to tell her that we would have preferred our children's art instead.

Barbara, mother of
Danielle, 6

that are arts based. There seem to be reform movements toward the arts. For example, after a twenty-year absence, the city of New York recently mandated a return of the arts to all elementary schools. Why? Because attendance at cultural institutions is an important source of revenue. They know that adults who haven't had arts training and arts backgrounds won't go to these places. There's a movement, but it's very hard to know exactly what's going on in individual schools. It is, however, universally true that in most public schools, the first thing that gets cut is the arts.

What do we lose when the arts aren't taught?

Cutting our children off from the arts is leaving them out of a conversation that continues within and across culture, across time and space. Art gives our children the opportunity and the tools to participate both as makers and perceivers in this important tradition that connects human beings across a number of different settings, circumstances, and periods of time. At a time when technology is rampant, the arts remind us of the importance of the *human* spirit. To leave them out, to give up the music room because you have forty new computers to bring in, is a very sad statement that leaves a worrisome legacy to our children.

For preschool children coming to school, to keep the arts out of the schools tells them that what they know how to do instinctively doesn't really matter here. A teacher can say, "I won't include the arts in my classroom because I'm not an artist," and parents respond, "Oh, that's okay." But if the teacher were to say, "I'm so sorry, we're not going to be doing math in the first grade because I'm not really much of a mathematician," parents will say, "Forget that, you'll find a way to teach math."

What can parents do to keep their children interested in art?

The great challenge is to keep children drawing through what we call the literal stage, ages eight through eleven, into

Colin's teacher was impressive. Using websites, her computer, and a projection screen, she showed the children paintings from museums throughout the world. When Colin drew a picture—that looked like a blue and green blob—for my father and he asked what it was, Colin said, "water lilies like mayonnaise [Monet's]."

Yale, father of
Colin, 7, and
Niles, 10

adolescence. Parents should have art supplies of all different kinds. Art supplies can be anything. You can put flour and water together to make dough or clay or use food coloring for paints. Give your children the opportunity to keep creating and make time for it at home. Art is very relaxing for children. They get into a flow of being totally engaged in what they are doing.

Before- and After-School Programs

- -

Since our daughter attended an afternoon kindergarten class, three days a week she went to the before-school program. The only problem was that unless we paid extra for enrichment classes, it was purely a baby-sitting service.

Tuan, father of Erin, 7, and Duy, 11

I talked to a number of people about the before- and after-school programs at their kids' schools. They all agreed that the "before" part of the equation was not a problem. For the most part, at least for children in morning kindergarten, the before-school program provides a safe haven for working parents to drop off their children before school starts.

The after-school component is different. I was told that in circumstances where the program is run by elementary school personnel, the quality usually is better. The similarity between programs—across the country—is that kindergartners are usually separated from the larger school population. They are assigned to classrooms that are solely for kindergartners. If the school is a large one and there is a separate kindergarten playground, that's where the kids play.

The children's activities are usually dependent upon whether the school offers part-day or full-day kindergarten. If it's a half-day program and school ends somewhere around noon, the kindergartners are usually alone with the after-school staff members for a few hours before the older children arrive. This allows the counselors time to concentrate on the kindergartners' needs, and some of the programs are a continuation of kindergarten. Once the first- through sixth-grade children arrive, while the kindergartners still are separated, the program may not be as strong since there generally is not an increase in staff, and the total number of children may quadruple.

A friend, Walt, whose child has been in a child-care environment since birth, and later in an after-school program, shared some insight.

"For Sam [his son], the problem was that his initial child-care program was way better than the program at his elementary school. The former program is known throughout the state, as is the director. It's attached to the university where I work, and the staff is great. For the most part, they are either people who are getting a degree in early childhood development, or undergraduates who work part-time and love kids. The program is developmentally appropriate for each age level.

"So when Sam began attending his elementary school's program, there was a huge difference for us. While that program is considered good, it didn't compare to what he, or my wife and I, were used to. However, the elementary school kindergarten program still is better than it is in other grades, and many of our friends whose children attend are happy with it.

"The curriculum is an extension of the kindergarten curriculum. They make art projects, play with blocks and other developmentally appropriate materials, and have a good time. Once Sam got over the initial sense of loss, because he missed the teachers at the child-care facility he had attended since birth and didn't find this program as interesting, he adjusted very well. Many of his friends from kindergarten attended the after-school program, and he also met children from other kindergarten classes.

"From what I hear from friends, our elementary school program is among the best. Some schools contract the programs out and don't oversee the quality control. So, I guess, as far as things go, we should feel lucky.

*O*n *the first day of kindergarten, my son, David, told me he got lost on his way to the after-school program. He mournfully said, "Mommy, I was standing there and I lost my teacher." I freaked; the director told me it was David's fault because he didn't follow the other children in line. Without blinking, I pulled him out of the program and found alternate care.*

Lauren, mother of
David, 7, and
Marshall, 9

"Another element for us is the summer program. For the first few years, Sam attended the summer program at his school. Again, he liked playing with his friends. There were some fun activities and field trips, which initially made my wife, Betsy, a nervous wreck, so Sam wasn't permitted to go. Betsy had nightmares that Sam would get lost at some amusement park and no one would know he was gone until it was time to leave. But a few weeks into the program, Sam begged us to let him go on the field trips.

"To allay some of her fears, Betsy and I took a few days off from work and alternately volunteered to help supervise. When we saw how responsible the aides were, that the children all wore camp T-shirts with their names on them and were constantly counted as they left each activity, we both felt better.

"I guess our only remaining question is the long-term effect of child care and after-school care on Sam's life. I don't think there have been any longitudinal studies of what the impact is. I do know that he's well socialized and likes to play with other kids. He does well in school and doesn't have any more behavioral problems than other kids his age. But every once in a while, after Betsy or I pick Sam up at 6:00 at night, and he looks tired and hasn't even started his homework because he finds it too difficult to concentrate, we have those moments when we don't know whether all this time spent away from home will have a long-term deleterious effect.

"God, I hope not."

Choosing an After-School Program

Wendy Schwartz is the editor of "A Guide to Choosing an After-School Program," the document from which this article has been adapted. Copyright permission is granted through the ERIC Clearinghouse on Urban Education from the Teachers College of Columbia University, New York, New York.

Fortunately, there are good after-school programs in most urban communities. Some may even be free; the cost of others is usually based on family income, and there may be subsidies or scholarships available. Schools run some programs themselves, and others are sponsored by schools or school districts. One advantage of having the after-school program located at the school that your children attend is that they don't have to travel to another location. Another is the availability of good facilities, such as a kitchen and gymnasium, and good equipment, such as a laboratory and computers. A disadvantage is that your children may feel like they just have a longer school day instead of a different, exciting experience in the afternoon.

Experienced community organizations, such as churches, boys and girls clubs, and "Y"s, run programs. Less formal programs include those run by day-care centers that open their doors to school-age children before and after school, and licensed family child-care providers. Independent programs may be held where the operator has its headquarters or runs other youth programs, or in a rented or donated space.

You know, it's been over ten years since my child attended kindergarten. I still feel guilty that I had to put him in a before- and after-school program. I was a single mother. What could I do?

Paula, mother of
Esteban, 18

CHECKLIST FOR FINDING AN AFTER-SCHOOL PROGRAM

1. Does the staff consist of responsible and caring adults who really like children and who can provide support and guidance? Is supervision adequate?

2. Is the program in a safe and clean environment? Is there enough space for activities and quiet time? Are the restrooms adequate? Is the space decorated in an inviting way?

3. Are nutritious snacks or meals provided?

4. Are there good resources, such as a library and sports equipment?

5. Do the activities look exciting and challenging? Are they age appropriate? Are the participants having fun as well as learning?

6. Are the activities those that your children like or want to learn?

7. Does the program coordinate group and individual learning with the school to be sure that participants benefit as much as possible from it?

8. Can children come before school and on holidays as well as in the afternoon? Is there an extra fee for that? Is there a late fee if you have to pick up your children after the program is over?

9. Can children attend only a few times a week instead of every day to accommodate parents' schedules or to save on costs?

10. What are the costs? Are there extra fees for trips, personal tutoring, and lessons?

Parent Participation

Our school's program was good. The director was outstanding. The teachers were kindergarten aides and they already knew the children. So the transition was easy.

Len, father of
Greg, 9, and
Cassie, 13

Parent involvement in after-school programs is just as important as in other aspects of children's lives. Good programs will ask parents what they want and need, and what their children want to learn and like to do, even before the children enroll.

It is important to keep in touch with the program staff after your children begin participating, to stay informed about how they are doing, and to find out if you can help your children learn more or get greater enjoyment. Since the children in most programs represent many cultures, it is useful for parents to talk to staff about their children's needs, their own child-rearing methods, and their expectations, to prevent conflicts and to help staff better appreciate diversity. By providing information about their culture and family history, parents can help staff offer the children a multicultural education.

Good programs also help parents participate in their children's development and education by arranging family activities at convenient times and organizing group sessions with staff that cover a variety of parenting issues. Children who see their parents become involved in activities sponsored by the after-school schedule will believe that the events are worth the effort of participation.

Bilingual Education

On the first day of
class, my wife and I
filled out the student
information card and wrote
that Spanish and English
were spoken in our home.
A week later, when I
picked up Marie from
school, I was shocked to
find that despite the fact
that she spoke perfect
English, she'd been placed
in an "English as a second
language" program. It
took a few days to sort out
the problem.

Santos, father of
Marie, 9

Alex grew up with Ramón, whose mother, Carla, took care of both boys three days a week while I wrote at my office. For three years, Alex and Ramón (who was five months younger) participated in their own multicultural learning experience. Carla, who is bilingual, talked, sang, and read to the boys in both English and Spanish. They napped together, ate together, and when they were older, played together.

Once Alex started preschool, Carla got a full-time job with another family. Still, we kept in touch and arranged play dates for the boys. A few months after Ramón and Alex started kindergarten (Ramón at a neighborhood parochial school), Carla called, with great concern.

"Ramón is not doing well in school," she said, with a huge sigh.

"Why not?" I asked in surprise.

"He is punished every day."

"For what?"

"He will not do anything they say. He pretends he does not speak English," she explained.

"So why don't they speak to him in Spanish?" I logically asked. "Don't the other kids speak Spanish?"

"Yes, but the teachers want them to speak English."

"Haven't these people heard of bilingual education?" I rhetorically asked.

"What should I do?"

"Talk to the principal. Tell her how you feel. If she won't let him speak Spanish, find another school. He's acting out because he's angry."

"I know."

"Carla, you sent Ramón to this school because you thought it would be safer than public school, and they offer a full-day schedule. It's not working out."

"No."

"What's the local public school like?"

"I don't know. It is big. The kids are . . ." she paused. "What will I do with him after school?"

I sighed. I didn't know what to say. Three weeks later, it became a moot point. Ramón was expelled because another kid called him a name in Spanish and Ramón called him a worse name in English. How ironic, I thought. Now Ramón was being punished for speaking English. The next time Carla called me, Ramón was already enrolled in the local public school, which not only offered a bilingual program but also an integrated multicultural curriculum. Her sister-in-law, who had young children at home, had agreed to take care of Ramón after school. Carla and I both felt that Ramón would finally be okay.

And so he is.

I n our school, many of the children come from China, Japan, Vietnam, and Korea. While the goal is to teach them English, can you image how confusing it is not only to live in a foreign country but also to try to learn the subject matter without any help in your native language?

Sakoto, mother of
Rose, 1, Oscar, 3,
and Hirotaka, 6

A Successful Approach to Learning English

Although bilingual education has been implemented in classrooms for twenty-five years in the United States, not everyone understands how it works. People have questions regarding the use of the home language in teaching students: How can they experience success with instruction in English when they spend so much time learning in Spanish? Won't they fall behind in their academic studies? These results are hard to witness directly.

When taught only in English, students may experience frustration at not being able to communicate even their most basic needs to their teachers. At the same time, they are unable to show how smart and ready to learn they are. Teachers see only that they are unable to complete work at their grade level.

In contrast to this, students in bilingual classes feel comfortable, among familiar surroundings, as they begin to tackle the unfamiliar English language. Also, during this early stage of development, students must experience success and learn about what they can do well. Teachers in bilingual classrooms recognize that students know one language and are in the process of learning English.

Finally, students continue learning in their home language while they develop their English language skills. This permits continued communication with parents and grandparents who may not know English. These are very good reasons to enroll your non-English-proficient child in a bilingual program, but several more important reasons are revealed through recent research results.

During the past twenty years, many research studies have been done on the effects of bilingual education. Some research studies have compared it to programs that use more English. Others compare student achievement with that of students in late-exit bilingual education programs (lasting five to seven years). They found that in late-exit bilingual programs

- Students did not fall behind in learning content-area subjects. After four or five years, they were making rapid gains, getting closer to the achievement levels of students whose first language was English.

When our grandparents and others came to this country, they all learned how to speak English. I think that if people come to this country to become American citizens, they should be taught in English.

Billy, father of
Earl, 6 months,
Sally, 4, and
William Jr., 7

- They learned English well. The greatest gains made by students were in mathematics, English language skills, and English reading.

- Parents of these students were able to provide them with homework assistance (since it was in the home language).

These academic goals were met because the home language creates a linguistic base. This language base serves as a stepping stone to learning English in an almost automatic way. Much of what is learned in the home language transfers automatically to the second language (English).

Researchers including James Cummins have concluded that success in learning a second language depends on a student's home language level of development. This explains how it is possible for someone having high levels of Spanish language development to learn English not only faster but also with better results. It makes sense to use such a positive and successful approach to teach both English and academic subjects!

In kindergarten, we enrolled our daughter in a Spanish immersion program. All our friends were sure she'd never learn how to speak Spanish. By the fourth grade, she was bilingual. In Los Angeles in the twenty-first century, I believe it's imperative that everyone learn how to speak Spanish.

Janet, mother of
Lorna, 9, and
Ted, 14

Choosing a School

In determining where his oldest child should go to school, Kin, a computer programmer for a large corporation, spent one full year accumulating data.

"That is the way I make decisions," said Kin. "Bonnie is our oldest child. She has two younger sisters. I need to pick a school that all three children can attend. Stephanie [who manages the college relations department at the same company], our children, and I live in a central location. I mapped a twenty-five-mile radius around our house. We are narrowing the choices."

"Kin leaves nothing to chance," Stephanie explained. "I visited a number of neighborhood schools and found one I like. But Kin has been charting test scores, reading citywide rankings, calling to find out teacher-pupil ratios, and asking about the educational level and experience of the teachers. By the time he's finished pestering people, no school will want to enroll our children," she said with a laugh.

We live in a rural area in Texas. There is one school, so that's the one we chose.

Joe, father of Jeff, 5, Danny, 10, and Sam, 12

Turning to me, Stephanie continued, "Kin is a first-generation American and I am a Sansei [third generation]. In Japan, the schools require so much of the children. If they don't do well throughout their school career, and don't test well, they won't be allowed to attend college. Although Kin came to this country when he was fifteen and attended college here, he can't forget how it is in Japan."

"We both want our children to go to good schools, graduate from fine colleges, and get good jobs," Kin said. "We disagree about the definition of a 'good' school. To me, it is all a matter of numbers," Kin explained. "Data is reliable. I know friends from work and from our church whose children attended schools that were too liberal, graduated from college without having a direction, and now have low-level jobs. I will not allow that for my children."

"*Our* children," Stephanie softly reminded him. "Because of our backgrounds, Kin and I look at life in different ways," Stephanie said. "My parents are as conservative as Kin. They wanted me to be a science major. I rebelled, graduated as a psychology major, and got a master's degree in psych as well. I love my work, but my parents are disappointed in my choices. In the last ten years, the only thing they think I've done right is to marry Kin."

Her eyes twinkled. "Anyway, my focus on finding a school is people-oriented. I rarely depend on numbers to make a decision. What I care about are enthusiastic teachers, nice children, and involved parents."

"I am more interested in a school where the goals of the teachers and principal are academic excellence, order, and self-discipline," Kin said.

"We'll see," said Stephanie as she looked at me and shrugged.

"Still, I am very proud of my wife, and I want our daughters to be scientists only if they want to," Kin said. Stephanie beamed in response.

"If not, they can become mathematicians," he said with a wink.

Effective Schools

George H. Wood is a high school principal, author of *Schools That Work* and *A Time to Learn,* and founder of the Institute for Democracy in Education. He is married to a kindergarten teacher.

What are the criteria for schools that work?

The best schools are small schools with about four or five hundred students per building. Evidence shows that children who go to small schools are more successful. Class size is another consideration. A recent study out of Tennessee and Iowa tracked a group of children for more than twenty years. They found that kids in smaller classes did better all the way through school regardless of their socioeconomic status. Schools that put a deliberate effort into keeping kindergarten and lower-grade classes small and intimate are probably schools that are having more success with kids as they move through the grades. The ideal number of students per kindergarten teacher ought to be about fifteen.

The second criterion to consider is whether the school is focused on authentic student work rather than external criteria. The emphasis should be on the quality of work students are given at each grade level rather than how effectively they can be taught to score on standardized tests. When you visit a school, look closely at what is on the walls. Is it genuine student work or is it twenty-seven colored-in Mickey Mouses or Donald Ducks?

The third criterion is the level of personalization between teachers, students, and parents. How well do teachers know their students? By what means is the school providing the opportunity for parents and teachers to build a partnership? Usually, schools provide the linkage through parent-teacher conferences, but there are much more powerful ways of establishing these relationships. Providing time for home visits is one. My wife is a kindergarten teacher. In her school, the kids stay home on Wednesdays. This enables the

Without visiting any schools but the ones in our neighborhood, my wife's and my parents sent us to our local elementary schools. We did the same with our kids. At last count, my brother and sister-in-law, who are older parents, have visited a half-dozen schools. We don't get it.

Al, father of
Amanda, 8 months,
and Ricky, 5

teachers to bring samples of the students' work to their homes and work with their parents. It's terrific. My wife knows all the children in her classroom and she knows their families.

Yet another method is pods, kindergarten through second grade. The children stay with the same teacher for three years so that the teacher really knows his or her students and their families.

In summary, the three criteria I look for in a school are size, authentic work, and personalization.

Is there a backlash against standardized testing?

I hope so. A lot of people rely on standardized test scores to predict future success for children in school. In fact, there is a great deal of research that indicates there are some more powerful predictors: size of school, number of adults involved in the child's life, attendance at school, family support. All those are bigger predictors than standardized test scores of long-term success both in college and in life. Yet we totally rely on tests to tell us standard things about non-standard children.

What should parents look for in terms of a school's educational philosophy?

The purpose of kindergarten should be to develop within children a love of learning, rather than a feeling that education means memorization. I have seen kindergartens that send home lists of what children should know by the end of the year, whether it is learning their letters or tying their shoes. These schools have achievement standards even though we know that children come into kindergarten with different maturation levels. Some children who do not even know their letters until the end of first grade are reading fluently by the end of third grade.

What you have to remember is that most kindergarten children cannot wait to start school. Yet by fourth or fifth grade many of them cannot wait to stop. Something happens to them. Until kindergarten, children learn at incredible rates.

Since a child's kinder-garten experience is crucial in terms of his or her educational and emotional development, we carefully researched a number of different schools—both public and private—to determine where to send our oldest child. We decided upon a private school which we thought would fully satisfy her academic, social, and aesthetic needs. And it has. Fortunately or not, once we immersed ourselves into the private school world, we felt it was the best place for our other children.

Anne, mother of
Kelly, 5, Boyce, 7,
and Lindsay, 8

Information flies at them and they catch it. They learn how to talk, walk, and interact without any instruction. Then we send them to school and say, "Well, forget about how you've figured things out until this point. Now we're going to do math for twenty minutes every day." The type of schedule is inconsistent with the way five-year-olds learn. By nature, they are inquisitive unless they are emotionally, physically, or psychologically damaged. The philosophy you look for is "How are we going to engage children in enjoying and loving to learn?" I would be wary of a school that gives you a list of activities kindergartners are expected to perform and the time frame in which they are to carry out these tasks. That would be a red light for me.

What I want to know is, when you talk about doing science, does that mean the teacher is going to take the children on walks in the neighborhood, let them look at leaves and roll around in them, and talk about why they fall off trees? That is science for a kindergarten child. It is not talking about photosynthesis. Kindergartners can't even pronounce the word. When you talk about community, does that mean the kids are going to go walk through their neighborhood, look at the different types of houses, and talk to or about who lives there? I always look for a teacher whose focus is oriented toward a child's world. We tend to believe that children think like adults, but that is not the case. We shouldn't worry about how much information children have accumulated by the end of kindergarten. Our concern should be whether learning is still fun.

The next important component is books, books, and books. Kids need to be read to. They must have books to take home. In my wife's kindergarten class every child takes a book home every night. They pick out a book that they've heard her read. They can't read these books themselves, but they can talk about them. The issue is not whether the children are able to read. The point is to encourage their parents to read to them. By the way, the only homework that should ever be assigned in kindergarten is for the parents to read to their children or to do enjoyable things such as collect leaves in the yard or take a walk and count houses.

How do you find out if a school is successful, whether teacher morale is high, and if the children are given an abundance of chances to learn?

Try to avoid using traditional measures. Every school district publishes test scores and other achievement-oriented material. But what I encourage parents to do, prior to their children going to kindergarten, is invite themselves to spend a day at school. You wouldn't buy a car without test driving it several times. People spend twenty to thirty hours shopping for cars. They use the Internet, go to dealerships, talk to their friends. Yet they'll rely on a five-minute visit to a classroom to decide what school their child should attend. You need to invest time—and the best way to find out about the school is to invite yourself to come spend the day.

Now if the school administrators say you can't visit, you should look more closely at the school. You can set them at ease by saying, "Look, I'm not coming here to test you, I just want to see what the school is like and what my child will be learning." Use the car analogy, "I wouldn't buy a car without a test drive. I'm not going to send my child to school without checking it out." That may mean you have to take a day off work, but how could you better spend your time than investing it in your child's education?

Most good teachers welcome visits from parents. The best teachers hope to have children in their classrooms whose parents make the effort to visit the school because they know that these parents are going to be involved. As I said earlier, one of the best predictors of children's success is whether their parents participate in their schooling; it makes all the difference.

We had two of our three children when we moved to a new city. We checked out different neighborhoods and rented a house in one with the best elementary school.

Ronnie, father of Bobby, 23 months, Sally, 5, and Ruthie, 7

Classrooms

"I was a little obsessed with the aesthetics of the classrooms," Jill, an attractive thirty-something mother of two told me.

"A little obsessed?" her husband, Seth, responded with a hearty laugh and turned to me. "How would you classify a woman who visits four different schools and comes home with pen-and-ink sketches of eight classrooms?"

I smiled but demurred as they continued their playful banter. "Okay," Jill admitted. "It was a little over the top, but I have a degree in architecture."

"So we visited our local elementary school," Seth interrupted, "and while the building itself is nondescript, the classrooms are cheerful. There's kids' art on the walls. They've got three computers per classroom, and in one class, there are animals. Lots of them. Hamsters, snakes, mice, and fish."

"It was nice," Jill said, "but I was equally interested in the square footage per child, the ergonomics of the desks and chairs, the quality of light, openness of space, colors, airiness, cleanliness of the bathrooms, and playground facilities."

Without a breath, she continued. "I wanted the environment to allow for creativity, exploration, and curiosity. Yet, I didn't want it to be overstimulating or too cluttered."

Seth laughed aloud. "Wanna hear the punch line?"

When my son was in kindergarten, I had no idea that the room was set up in any specific way. When my friend said, "Aren't the learning centers great?" I said, "What are you talking about?" Gosh, did I feel dumb.

Robin, mother of Patrick, 8

I nodded. Jill shook her head and wanly smiled.

"After all Jill's hard work, when our son Spencer came home from school and Jill asked him whether he had a nice day, he said, 'My teacher's nice. I held a hamster. Our class is in a refrigerator truck.'"

"'A what?' I asked, assuming that I had misunderstood him," Jill said.

"'A great big refrigerator truck,' he slowly enunciated." Seth is now howling with laughter. I'm totally confused and have no idea what they're talking about until Jill explains.

"Spencer meant that his classroom was a bungalow. During the summer before school started, they added bungalows so that they could satisfy the then-new California reduced class-size requirement."

"It turns out it was all for the best," Seth added. "The main building is hot from spring through the fall, and these bungalows are air-conditioned. That's why Spencer thought he was in a refrigerator truck."

Jill shrugged her shoulders and smiled. "That night, my parents called from New York to ask Spencer about his first day of school and he proudly told them that his classroom was a refrigerator truck. My mother laughed and my father said, 'Only in L.A.'"

The Importance of the Classroom Environment

Barbara Thompson, Ph.D., is an associate professor and faculty coordinator for Early Childhood Education in the Special Education Department at the University of Kansas.

The classroom should be an environment that has been thoughtfully and carefully designed for kindergarten children. The appearance of a room has a major impact on learning. Children feel good when their classroom is aesthetically pleasing and child-centered. They develop a sense of importance when their materials, posters, paintings, and writing samples are placed at their eye level. Children like classrooms that have a sense of order.

The kinds of activities that children can engage in is heavily influenced by the classroom setup. Are they able to sit on the floor? Is the room designed for small and large group activities?

I also look for basic safety requirements. Are the outlets covered with protectors? Are the objects safe? Have the children been properly taught how to handle tools, such as scissors? Do they know the procedures for fire drills and other school emergencies?

Another important classroom element is the learning materials. Have they been carefully chosen? Has the teacher thought about their impact on the children's learning experience? Are the supplies well cared for? Broken crayons and pencils or puzzles with missing pieces carelessly tossed into a storage bin send a message as well.

Personally, I prefer environments where children are allowed to make choices and actively participate in their own learning experience. When the teacher directs all the activities and the children are required to do everything in unison, what lesson are they learning? In the long term, how will this method of teaching affect the children's decision-making skills?

I sometimes feel like I'm from a different planet. Everything about kindergarten, whether it's the physical education, the rooms, or the music has some sort of educational purpose.

March, mother of
Simon, 6

Kindergarten Centers

Jenna Thorsland taught kindergarten for three years in Reynolds Upper School in Upper Saddle River, New Jersey, and is now a first-grade teacher at Siomac School in Wyckoff, New Jersey.

THE WRITING CENTER

The writing center should be set up with all kinds of interesting materials to encourage writing. The children can either self-select a topic to write about or the teacher may assign a topic, such as a theme or unit they are learning about. The children work independently at sounding out the words they would like to write and may choose to consult a picture dictionary, or *pictionary,* or a wordbook if one is available. The children will also learn about writing for an audience if at the end of center time the teacher chooses to have children share what they've written.

THE READING CENTER

In the reading center, children can read a book independently or with a friend. They can choose books they are interested in and reread old favorites. Reading with a friend encourages social development. While the children are reading together or looking at the pictures in a book, they are often discussing the book and illustrations. The reading center may also include a basket of familiar and unfamiliar poems that the children can read. The rhyme and predictability of many short poems help to foster phonemic awareness.

GAMES

The children can learn all sorts of concepts through reading games and math games, depending on which concepts the teacher likes to have the children independently practice. They can work on matching uppercase and lowercase letters, putting numbers in order, practicing handwriting skills, or doing addition. By having the children work individually on these games, the teacher is better able to challenge students who are more advanced and allow additional practice for those who have difficulty with a concept. The games area may also include commercial games such as Candy Land, Don't Break the Ice, or others to encourage social interaction among the children, or Legos or Lincoln Logs to encourage small motor development as well as social skills.

I am impressed by how the classroom environment supports the learning experience.

Bill, father of
Ria, 5

DRAMATIC PLAY

The dramatic play area allows students the opportunity to role-play, work through problems, play cooperatively with other children, and further develop social skills. The center may be set up as a house, or may change throughout the year depending on what the class is learning about. In February during Dental Health Month, for example, the center may be transformed into a dentist's office. Changing the center piques the children's interest and enables them to role-play other situations. It will also encourage children who do not usually choose the dramatic play area to try it.

THE SCIENCE CENTER

At the science center, children can explore and manipulate a variety of science materials, which may include shells, seeds, rocks, or other items. Using a magnifying glass, they can choose to take a closer look and make observations of objects. Depending on the types of materials, the children may be able to predict what would happen to an object over time. For example, they might guess what will happen if an apple is left out for a week. While the class is learning about a particular subject, the children may be allowed to bring in materials, such as leaves. They can also read and look at the illustrations or photographs in science books.

THE BLOCK CORNER

In the block corner, the children build various types of structures. They can work cooperatively or independently to build tall structures where they will need to use their knowledge of balance in order to make the structure stand. Often, children enjoy working cooperatively at the block center because they can build bigger and better structures with the help of others. Working cooperatively in this center enhances social development.

COMPUTERS

Many classrooms are now equipped with computers, which can enhance the kindergarten program. There are many educational software programs that can help children develop skills in many academic areas. Children can work independently at the computer or computers, or they may work cooperatively in pairs in order to foster social development.

Computers

I'm a "techie," so I was thrilled when I found out our neighborhood elementary school had a program for kindergartners. When I saw the new computer lab, filled with state-of-the-art equipment, I wanted to quit my job and hang out with the kids.

Tracy, mother of
Ellen, 7, and
Ted, 9

For over a decade, I had no personal philosophy about computers. I owned the same one for thirteen years. It had no bells and whistles; I used it only for word processing. When Alex started kindergarten, everything changed. His public school was big on technology. There was not only a computer lab, but also four computers in every classroom.

From day one, Alex and the machines bonded. He not only got "it," but he was good at it, and loved it. This child of ours who (until then) had been raised with very little television, no video games, books and more books but no electronics, suddenly became a digital kid overnight.

Oddly enough, I didn't think very much about the philosophical ramifications of early computer usage. I figured computing was a good skill to learn. The school had a great program. They understood the importance of hiring a technology specialist to teach the kids and the teachers. They didn't believe in buying drill and skill programs—which kids do by rote and which eventually can bore them to tears.

Instead, Alex's school invested in three interactive packages—which means the kids actually have to think, create, and make choices when using the computer. One program includes word processing, spreadsheets, databases, painting, drawing, and communications. Another is a great high-end computer graphics program. The third enables the children to use "hyperstacks" (think of it as electronic cards) to develop multimedia presentations.

The bottom line, that I didn't consider when Alex was in kindergarten, is whether the cost of computers, in time and money, is worth the return. Each school has a finite budget, and if a portion is spent on computers, it's taken away from something else. There are only so many hours in the day for "extras," and someone must decide whether that time is devoted to music, art, or computing. There are dozens of other important issues relating to intelligence, brain development, critical thinking, literacy, gender, health, and safety, and the resolution is neither obvious nor easy.

From a personal perspective, now that Alex is eleven and is known for his computer prowess, his skills amaze me. In the third grade, he produced a newsletter on *The Tempest* in which he wrote all the articles, designed the columns, imported clip art, chose the colors, and picked all the fonts (typefaces). He knows how to use the Internet for school research as well as for downloading games. He has designed greeting cards that are creative and clever. But it has taken an enormous amount of time to get that good, time that might have been spent elsewhere.

One evening I received a call from a friend of mine who was evaluating two private elementary schools for her kindergartner. Her child had been accepted at both, and she and her husband were agonizing over their decision. One school had a state-of-the-art computer program, and the other a children's chorus and orchestra.

Having talked with her many times on the subject, I couldn't believe she had any questions left. This time she asked, "How do you know computers are good for kids?"

I paused a moment and reflected. She had never asked the question quite that way. "There isn't enough research and there are no definitive answers," I finally said. "There's a great

If I could have signed a petition saying I didn't want my son to begin using a computer in kindergarten, I would have. But I knew it would make him hate me.

Julie, mother of
Jake, 8

schism between technology supporters and detractors. I can't tell you what to do."

That night as I was putting Alex to bed, I casually asked for the hundredth time, "Are you sure you don't want to play a musical instrument?"

"No," he replied and rolled his eyes. "You've been talking to moms about your book again."

"Yeah," I admitted.

He shook his head, sighed, and went to sleep.

Young Children and Computers

Alan C. Kay, Ph.D., formerly a fellow at Apple Computer, and a founder of the Xerox Palo Alto Research Center, is Vice President for Creative Technology at Disney Imagineering.

Maria Montesorri, one of the keenest observers of children's development and a major influence on Jean Piaget (known for his pioneering work on the development of intelligence in children), pointed out that children are set up and driven by nature to learn the world around them through play. If we want them to grow up in the twentieth century, then we should give them twentieth-century toys and environments to play in, not try to force them into a poor caricature of university-style classrooms.

Piaget, as well as educators John Dewey, Lev Vygotsky, and Jerome Bruner, would additionally agree with her that the main task of childhood learning in the twentieth century is to go beyond gaining the common sense of a traditional society to develop the "uncommon sense" that provides the context and heuristics (problem-solving techniques) to deal with modern ideas in relation to the world, including science and governance.

An important result gained from careful observation of children is that they are not "imperfect adults that need to be fixed," but that their thinking processes during their normal development are often quite different from adult thought, and, especially, that there are certain kinds of adult thinking that are almost impossible for very young children.

Bruner's way to portray this has held up well for almost forty years: Three of the most important ways we have of knowing the world are through physical interaction, visual and auditory configurations, and by symbolic representations and logic. Children and adults can engage in all three, but most children are first dominated by physical interactions that form the basis for later figurative perception and thinking, which in turn form the basis for later symbolic thought.

Piaget thought that a child who was in the "visual stage" pretty much had to reason visually, but Bruner showed convincingly that such children who were then prevented from seeing the situation could think rather well—and quite differently!—about it using language and logic.

A good rule of thumb from these thinkers: If you don't have a good known-to-work approach to learning something, start with physical interactions, move to visual and other figurative portrayals, and then try to capture the ideas in symbolic language, especially in the form of mathematics.

A simplistic application of this rule of thumb would require us to have kindergartners do things only in the physical world. But a more relaxed observation of development would notice that children also spend a lot of time learning to talk with each other, listening to stories, acting them out, making them up, looking at picture books, trying to read them, trying to write their names, and so on. It's all nicely mixed up. Perhaps a stronger way to apply these ideas would be to have lots of stuff going on but to make sure there is enough physical learning in early development, leading to the figurative, leading to the symbolic, and so on.

An important side observation is that children are essentially artists, that is, their actual motivations are deeply connected to emotional satisfaction from being a maker. As Cesare Pavese said: To know the world, one must construct it.

If one accepts these ideas as a starting place for helping children develop, then many different paths of thought would suggest that children and television be kept well separated for many years. One way to think of this is that television's way to engage with humans is as an image and thought prosthetic. If you put a prosthetic on a healthy limb, it withers.

The computer is trickier to think about, in part because it can imitate other media so well and most of its content is simply borrowed in various ways. The above remarks about television certainly apply to the computer when it is being used to imitate representations similar to television.

Computing is hard to evaluate in that almost no one really understands what it is about, including most people who think they know what "computer literacy" is and advocate for or against it. Jonathan Swift would say there is a kind of "confederacy of dunces" dance going on right now.

At the beginning of the twenty-first century, the computer will be most interesting and important when it is used like a dynamic book, representing the kinds of deep ideas that can be represented in books but in a kind of "live language." Here, all the things we think are important about reading, writing, literature of ideas, science, math, and politics can be even more strongly portrayed and learned by using a suitably set-up computer instead of a book: The computer can contain the best books we have and go beyond them.

Our society doesn't worry very much—and probably shouldn't—about the serious use of books in kindergarten, but neither do we have a really workable way to introduce the serious use of books to most children as they grow older. I think almost everyone would agree that it is good to have books in kindergarten but to not force very young children to read. Children need to have adults read to them so that they develop a sense of romance and mystery that good stories convey. Exposure to literature will encourage children to want to read. When their own parents read aloud to them or read silently to themselves, children begin seeing the relationship between the written and the spoken word.

Montesorri was very clever about creating precursor toys for reading and writing, including her famous sandpaper letters of the alphabet that helped children learn the shapes through physical interaction. Myself and others have experimented with tactile output devices (such as a mouse that lets you feel what's on the screen as you move your hand over it) so that the ideas of Montesorri, Piaget, and Bruner can be used with very young children.

There is every reason to believe that many of the same principles we apply to books and young children should apply to computers. For example, we should be concerned about what's in a book, but if the book is good we shouldn't worry if the child is solitary for a few hours while reading it. We want the children to be authors as well as consumers. The children need to start with stories, but we should help them gradually develop abilities in nonstory reading and writing, such as argumentative essays, and so on. We want to have books around even while the children play in the physical world.

It's pretty clear that most homes and schools at present are not sophisticated enough about computers (for many, even about books) to make use of them in growth-inducing and nondestructive ways. However, the gap is large enough between the semiliterate-in-print adult and the completely nonliterate-in-computing adult to say that, at present, most uses of computing by children are not helping them develop in the twenty-first-century world of important ideas. In fact, many uses of computers, as with television, are having the opposite effect; whereas, with the book, even semiliteracy among adults can be of some aid.

To me, the important difference between computers and television is that the world would generally be better off without television, but, as with books and reading and writing, we need to find ways to understand and teach the computer's great and new powers of expression. One of the most important tasks of the next few years is to invent and provide a real "children's computer" through which they can engage in real twenty-first-century play.

In our school, the children learn how to build things with wood, grow vegetables, and take care of animals. What do I think of technology? I try not to think of it at all.

Star, mother of Donovan, 6, and Jimi, 15

To Compute or Not to Compute

Jane M. Healy, Ph.D. and educational psychologist, is the author of *Failure to Connect: How Computers Affect Our Children's Minds—and What We Can Do About It* and *Endangered Minds: Why Children Don't Think and What We Can Do About It.*

Are computers good for kindergartners?

Under limited circumstances, computers can be useful. For children with special needs, computers offer many wonderful assisted technologies. For "normally" developing children, I am very skeptical about much use before age seven. Between the ages of five and seven, the brain experiences many rapid changes in which it firms up the learning of early childhood and gets ready for the more abstract-symbolic learning that comes later. In order to develop strong foundations, even five-year-olds still need a great deal of physical learning. This requires real-world, three-dimensional experiences, not sitting looking at a two-dimensional screen. Moreover, these ages are critical for child language and social development. Because computer use subtracts time from these activities, it risks jeopardizing both future learning and personal development. And this applies to both school and home.

What should parents look for in a kindergarten computer program?

First, parents should look for a curriculum that either does not include computers or where the computer does not dominate the program, where there is plenty of human language and social interaction, three-dimensional experience, and time off the computer. Second, they should look for teachers who understand why they are using a computer and how it's improving their curriculum rather than getting in its way. Third, they should make sure that basic safety guidelines are followed because, without them, computer use can be destructive to children's eyes and bodies. Fourth, they should make sure that their child is eager to engage in other activities, socialization, outdoor play, art, dance, and music.

In other words, you want to have the teacher and children, rather than computer techies, running the program and doing the thinking. So far the research has shown no advantages to using computers in kindergarten; little if any evidence justifies the time and money that we are spending on computers. For older students, of course, the situation may be different, and that's where most technology money should be going.

What concerns should parents have about computer use?

There are basically two risks you're running by exposing children to too much of this technology too soon. One is subtracting time from the brain's important need to do other things, to develop intelligence, sense of self, and personal skills. The second is that the wrong kind of software—games for example, or inappropriate Internet use—can actually embed faulty learning habits in the brain. Because so much of the input has already been programmed, the scope of learning tends to be narrow and reductive in the sense that there is only one right answer for a set pattern of responses. Moreover, too much fast-paced visual stimulation, without a lot of reflection and language accompanying it, can permanently disrupt language development. The child becomes more used to sitting and poking buttons and looking at things, as opposed to using his or her mind actively to figure out how to talk about something. This could affect social and reading comprehension skills later on.

What suggestions do you have for home usage?

- At this age your child should not be spending more than half an hour a day using a computer.

- Think very seriously before you buy a computer for a child under seven. In my opinion, they are better off without one.

Computers are the most exciting invention since automobiles. Our children have the capability of communicating with kids throughout the world. I can't imagine why anyone would discourage this kind of learning.

Donald, father of
Mark, 6

- If there is a family computer, kindergartners certainly are going to play with it, but I would not make the computer the child's own personal plaything.

- No five-year-old should have a computer in his or her room. Keep it in a central place where you can keep an eye on what your child is doing with it.

- When your child is on the computer, you should put a chair next to his or hers, sit down with the child, and be a part of the experience. If you feel like a techno-logic ignoramus, don't worry, you can learn a lot by simply watching. Don't turn children loose. Computers are not baby-sitters, and unless you are available to help your children, the computer can actually be more damaging than television.

- If you don't know anything about computers, you and your child can explore together.

- Be concerned about any Internet exploration unless you are right there and have previewed the websites that you and your child are going to visit.

- Talk to your child about the computer world. Children at this age particularly tend to believe that the computer is smarter than people are and that if the computer tells them to do something, they should do it. We need to start early talking to them about the fact that computers are only servants of human beings.

If parents and teachers limit the time usage for kindergarten kids, what's the big deal?

Walter, father of Peter and Darlene, both 7

Your job as a parent is to make sure there is a big dimension of humanity in your child's life, that computer use doesn't get in the way of normal activities, and that your child has plenty of time to exercise the body and play imaginatively. Even though computers are fun to play with, you need to get your child's mind and body away from the machine that can be so distracting from the real business of childhood.

Curriculum

- -

"So what's the current take on curriculum?" I asked my friend David. We've known each other for years and he is the father of three, the youngest of whom, Erin, recently finished kindergarten.

"Developmentally appropriate learning," he said, shrugging his shoulders. "Integrated thematic units. Broad yet complex levels of knowledge."

"Wow," I responded.

"What was your curriculum like in kindergarten?" David asked.

"We didn't use the word 'curriculum,' but it was the usual stuff."

"You played, sang songs, did finger painting, listened to stories, and napped?" he asked, with a smile on his face.

"My school was more sophisticated," I replied. "We sawed."

"You sawed?" he responded, sounding quite impressed.

"Yes. We planned our project, measured the wood, sawed it, and hammered everything together."

"You hammered?"

"We were precocious."

"What did you make?" David asked.

We live in techno-logical times. If our children don't start learning more math and science, they won't be able to compete.

Jerry, father of Lewis, 7, and Kristin, 9

"A cargo truck."

"How can you possibly remember after all these years?"

"My mother kept it. It's cute—kind of like a teepee on wheels."

He laughed aloud. "Why did it look that way?"

"I couldn't figure out how to cut the truck panels the same size. I had trouble hammering the nails, so I glued the panels together and they collapsed."

"Unbelievable," he said. "Did it ruin your self-esteem?"

"Of course not. I realized that each kid had different talents. Some knew how to measure better. Others were more artistic. Some had better small motor skills."

"You figured all this out in kindergarten?" he asked in awe.

"No. Twenty years later in therapy."

We both laughed.

"Today, parents would be more concerned with the curricular purpose of the assignment," David said. "Are there measurable results? Does it tie into a thematic unit like transportation? Did their child learn something new like mathematics through measurement? An appreciation for aesthetics? Mechanical or spatial skills? It's okay to a certain degree, but I think they overdo it."

"I agree. Still, how many cargo trucks can a kid make? Napping was a drag. We had a half-day schedule so it seemed like we napped a few hours after we'd awakened."

"Did you learn anything in kindergarten?"

"Yes! I learned that hammering and sawing are fun although they are not my forte. You might say I am 'woodworking challenged.'"

David nodded. "Do you know what a curriculum evaluation group would say about your truck?"

"What?"

"That it wasn't a good choice for an activity. It was not developmentally appropriate for you to use a saw. It was discriminatory because the program did not allow all the children to succeed."

Who cares whether kindergarten is academically or play-oriented? Good teachers have always known how to challenge their students.

Arlene, mother of Mary, 6, and Holden, 8

"Undoubtedly true. But we grew up in different times. Our teachers had different expectations."

"Like what?" David asked.

"They wanted us to learn life lessons. They taught us how to go to the bathroom in pairs. We became more adept in the sandbox and better at sharing. We learned a bunch of songs and made lots of new friends."

"Kind of like Robert Fulgham?"

"Exactly, but I think he must have learned more or he was able to articulate it better. *All I Really Need to Know I Learned in Kindergarten* was a bestseller for years."

"So, all in all, do you think your kindergarten experience was a successful one?"

"Yes! I learned to climb the jungle gym faster than anyone else."

"So what?" he quizzically countered.

"Isn't it obvious?"

"No."

"The jungle gym is a metaphor for life. Those who climb the fastest are the first ones to reach the top."

"Give me a break," he said, with laughter.

"You left yourself wide open," I answered with a twinkle in my eye.

*M*ost states have curricular standards of what children should learn in each grade. I'm surprised they are not routinely distributed each time your child enters a new grade.

Pamela, mother of Lisa, 5

An Integrated Approach to Learning

Carol Meyer, Ed.D., is the principal of Central Kindergarten Center, a school with seven hundred kindergartners, in Eden Prairie, Minnesota.

Central Kindergarten Center has incorporated an integrated, thematic whole language approach to presenting the curriculum in every classroom. In our program, each child is able to enjoy success by actively participating in hands-on activities, communicating in written format, and reading and understanding words at his or her own level.

All kindergartners have the opportunity to explore the world of print. Letters and letter sounds are taught and reinforced throughout the year. The students learn prereading and reading skills by listening to and reading quality literature, and learn the sounds and words in a meaningful context.

The program is activity oriented. The children learn by doing. They will be cooking, acting out stories, singing, collecting, creating, writing, painting, drawing, and investigating as they learn letters, sounds, and words. The teacher monitors each child and adjusts the program to meet his or her needs. For example, one child might be looking for and identifying the letter *s* in a given poem while another child may be reading the poem. All children are able to participate and be successful no matter what their developmental level in reading.

I came of age in the seventies and played throughout my entire undergraduate career. Why should my kid's kindergarten curriculum be less fun than my college one was?

Paul, father of Rafe, 7

Our program has a strong emphasis on writing. Children become aware of print by using it for a real and meaningful purpose. The children start early in the year to write on their own. The teachers understand that not all children will be at the same level. The emphasis is on the child's own ideas and the process of writing. In addition to their own writing, the children will be involved in dictating stories and helping write class stories.

Integration of our curriculum teaches the children to utilize skills learned from math, language arts, science, social studies, and health areas to deal with real-life situations. For example, while teaching a unit on caterpillars, we may study the metamorphosis of the caterpillar, learn about the types of flowers that attract butterflies, follow the flight of butterflies on a map, and write and illustrate a class book about gardens.

The kindergarten program has been developed to enable every child to participate and succeed, whatever his or her developmental level. Kindergartners will continue to acquire the concepts and strategies needed toward becoming successful readers and lifelong learners.

Kindergarten Themes

Natalie Thomas has been an elementary school teacher for fifteen years. She teaches at George H. Conley Elementary School in Roslindale, Massachusetts.

There are no hard-and-fast rules that indicate which themes should be studied in the kindergarten year. If each theme meets the following criteria, children will learn as much by focusing on "transportation" as they will on "farm animals."

■ The theme must be relevant, meaningful, and accessible to the interest and needs of the children. Children must have many opportunities to gather firsthand information about the subject. In an urban setting, "transportation" would be a more appropriate theme than "farm animals," unless the teachers are prepared to make field trips to a farm and/or bring animals into the classroom.

■ The theme content must be presented in a developmentally appropriate manner. Introducing the working of a diesel engine as part of a transportation theme would be inappropriate for children who must experience concrete examples in order to understand a concept. However, children can discuss why all forms of transportation need an energy source—animal, water, wind, or electrical power—in order to move.

■ The theme must be valid for the children. They must be able to recognize and apply the concepts, skills, and attitudes to their lives. It should be easy for children to talk about the theme and use their new skills both in and out of school. The theme must support and encourage the development of specific skills.

■ The subject matter must easily be integrated into the activity and content areas. The theme must be broad and complex enough to offer levels of knowledge and skill development, and to encourage the use of a variety of resources such as books, materials, people, and films.

I would hope that educators who develop kindergarten curricula have spent time with kindergarten children.

Lynne, mother of Kellie, 14 months, Gail 5, and Sean, 9

■ Each theme should encourage an awareness of cultural diversity, interdependence between people, and cooperative living.

A Good Mix

Lilian Katz is the director of the ERIC Clearinghouse on Elementary and Early Childhood Education and professor emerita at the University of Illinois at Urbana-Champaign.

Is the trend toward academics developmentally appropriate for kindergarten children?

It is difficult to give a flat "no." It helps to distinguish between the academic and the intellectual, as this differentiation, which most people ignore, is one of the most critical issues. Academic development focuses on learning that which children cannot discover by themselves. Someone has to help them learn the alphabet and how to write. Some kids learn to read and write more easily than others do, but generally children need help from adults.

Intellectual development encompasses children's inborn dispositions to make sense of their world, to try to understand cause and effect. "What happens if I do this? How high can I build a tower with blocks?" In other words, effective kindergartens, as well as preschools, support and stimulate children's intellectual development.

In kindergarten, some children are ready for some academic work. Many young kids enjoy learning to write, and some are ready to start some kind of reading. Almost all kindergartners are ready for what we call print awareness and prereading: rhyming and awareness of letter-to-sound correspondence (which in English is a big problem). So the question is, what is the best mix?

If you ignore intellectual development and concentrate on rote learning activities, many children psychologically tune out by about the second grade. Many people think that exer-

Computer education is usually considered an add-on rather than an integrated part of the curriculum. I wonder why?

Monty, father of Robinson, 6, and Margaret, 9

cises and drills develop children's intellectual powers, but they don't. They deaden them. On the other hand, kindergarten programs in which the kids just cut and paste are also intellectually insufficient.

For some time, I have been working with teachers, helping them involve children in what we call projects—investigations of life around them. Substantive projects. The kids are actually doing research, asking questions, and interviewing people. If they are studying the local supermarket, they interview people who work there and customers who shop there. They analyze information. There are some data supporting the effectiveness of these investigations and how they support children's natural intellectual dispositions. An academic environment that stresses exercises and drills is no better than an environment that emphasizes cutting and pasting.

Kindergartners need a mix of both academic and intellectual elements. A lot of good intellectual work is done by observing the natural environment: things that grow, how they grow, and how they don't. On the academic side, children can benefit from being encouraged to write their names, practice their emerging literary skills by writing real messages to give to others, and strengthen their emerging mathematical skills by counting things for particular purposes.

Evidence suggests that the damage of excessive academic pressure in kindergarten does not show up in kindergarten, but later. If you look at end-of-kindergarten test scores, kids who have had heavy academic pressure naturally do better because that is what's tested. But when you follow those children, by second or third grade they are behind because they have had enough.

As I have told the parents of my grandchildren, look for a kindergarten that is neither solely an introduction to academics, nor one where the emphasis is too heavily oriented toward play. Learning is meaningful when children use the skills they have and are encouraged to wrap their minds around a topic in some depth.

I'm not sure I understand the purpose of a structured curriculum for five- and six-year-olds.

Holly, mother of
Jared, 5

Daily Schedule

----

*O*ur school had a
half-day schedule,
which was a good thing for
our daughter. By the time
she finished three-and-a-
half hours of school, she
was ready to take a nap.

Susan, mother of
Katie, 7, and
Sean, 9

When Alex was in kindergarten, he started school at 8:00 A.M. and finished at 12:05 P.M. While his school day surely could have and undoubtedly should have been longer, neither the teachers nor most of the parents appeared obsessed by what the children accomplished on a daily basis.

Times have changed. Schools across the country are moving toward a full-day kindergarten schedule, in many cases for good reason. Independent of the length of the kindergarten day, I still think the quality of the program, as always, depends upon the quality of the teacher.

In one full-day classroom I visited, the schedule was tightly packed but flowed seamlessly. The teacher had a magnetic personality; the children were bubbling. When I arrived, there were three different math activities going on simultaneously; children were either counting popsicle sticks, putting blocks in patterns, or cutting out shapes from different colored paper. During my stay, two groups of eight kids were taken out of class (at different times) to work with science and music specialists. The music class was joyful. The kids collectively sounded like Ethel Merman. And in the science class, I learned more about types of cacti than ever before. During the history lesson I left because I felt bad that I didn't know as much about the Mayan civilization as a few of the five-year-olds sitting at my table.

In a half-day kindergarten classroom, the teacher reminded me of a military platoon leader. Her voice was clipped, and her pace was exacting. There were time slots for everything. The children read, wrote, and sang on command (in anticipation of an assembly, I was told). They had a twenty-minute recess, which was also the bathroom break, snack time, and art period. I couldn't believe the precision it took to funnel thirty-four children toward five easels where they were given three to five minutes to paint identical flowers. Those who sat quietly for snack time were rewarded with a small bag of popcorn. Since I had been well behaved, I got one too, but when the teacher turned her back, I disappeared without a trace. The stress was palpable. In the teacher's defense, she was responsible for teaching two half-day kindergarten classes back-to-back. No easy feat.

A religious school's schedule included two hours of religious training, although it was a full-day kindergarten so it was easily accommodated. In another full-day program, the kids and I were having so much fun with building blocks that I didn't want to leave. When the aide took the kids to recess, I asked the teacher, a veteran of the vagaries of changing school policies, about her educational philosophy.

"A few years ago, our half-day program was extended to a full day," she said, "but I teach the way I always have. My schedule is still based on the children's interests. If the children are entranced by a book I'm reading, we spend more time reading it. If they're having a wonderful time during free play or if we are experiencing the first snow of the season, our schedule, which is loose at best, shifts accordingly."

"And you're not concerned with how much the children accomplish?" I asked.

She smiled in response. "No matter what the so-called experts say, a successful kindergarten experience is not measured by quantifiable data. I'm more concerned with how the children learn to adapt to each other, to me, and to a new school environment. Are they excited by our class activities? Are they curious? Do they participate? Are they challenged? Kindergarten is the beginning of an extraordinary journey. While it's nice to have a longer day, the number of hours a child attends school does not ensure a program's quality."

That night I asked a friend, who had been a kindergarten teacher for years, why the kindergarten schedules were so different. "When I taught, a teacher had to cover a certain amount of material during the course of a year," she said. "How we organized it was our own responsibility. While there is an increasing pressure for accountability, there is still flexibility within the system."

"I'm troubled that there isn't more unstructured time," I said with concern. "When do kids get to scream their lungs out, walk around the school yard with no purpose in mind, eat worms, smack each other just because they feel like it, and grovel in the sand?"

"We're entering the twenty-first century," she replied with a laugh. "Nowadays, parents want their kids to be competitive in the marketplace so they can be lawyers, M.B.A.s, and run computer companies. Somehow groveling doesn't sound like great preparation."

"I'm not so sure about that," I said, chuckling as I hung up the phone.

Half-Day Kindergarten

Debbie Wong has taught kindergarten for fourteen years and currently teaches at Melvin Avenue Elementary School in Reseda, California.

Since I started teaching kindergarten, there have been many changes. Most dramatic of all is the reduction of class size from thirty-three children to twenty. However, class size reduction has come with the demand for more academic achievement. Now children are expected to read forty to fifty words in one minute without missing any words and to be able to retell a story by writing a complete sentence. These used to be first-grade skills.

The advantage of a half-day program is that it's an easier transition for children who have never been away from their parents. Spending fifteen minutes, rather than a longer period of time, in a learning center helps those children who are working to lengthen their attention span. When children are having a bad day, it's over much more quickly.

The advantage of a full-day schedule is that with increased pressure for academic performance, the extra time would diminish the stress for the children and me. We would be able to spend more time doing each activity. Other than center time, the children's day would not be delineated into ten- to fifteen-minute segments.

I felt a half-day schedule was a real waste. Because my wife and I both work, our children had gone to a full-time preschool. In kindergarten, they spent more time in the after-school program than they did in their own classroom.

Bob, father of
Donnie, 5, and
Sherry, 7

Our Daily Schedule

7:55–8:05	Look at books
8:05–8:15	Flag salute, attendance, calendar, and counting
8:15–8:30	Explanation of center work
8:30–9:30	Center time: language arts and reading readiness. The teacher oversees the children in the writing center and teaches phonics or beginning sounds activity. The children independently cut and paste. An aide leads a word-recognition activity.
9:30–10:00	Bathroom break, nutrition, recess, and outdoor activity
10:00–10:50	Math, art, science
10:50–11:05	Music, sharing, and story time
11:05–11:10	Explanation of homework
11:10–11:15	Review of day and dismissal

Full-Day Kindergarten

Addie Gibb teaches full-day kindergarten at Seneca Elementary
School in Seneca, Missouri.

I have been teaching kindergarten in a full-day setting for four
years now, and I really love it! Advantages include having a
smaller student load so that the teacher gets to know the students and their individual needs better. It is easier to recognize and remediate learning difficulties quickly, and there is
more time in which to plan remediation activities. Reporting
to parents can be more frequent and complete. The teacher
has the opportunity to keep more extensive anecdotal records
and portfolios. The longer day enables the students to complete activities at a more relaxed pace. It allows for more pro-
ject-based activities and more hands-on learning. There is
more time for student exploration.

The disadvantage of a full-day schedule is that adjustment
may take longer for those children who have not been in a
group setting. What's most important for everyone to realize
is that the purpose of the full-day schedule is not to foist on
children a watered-down version of first grade. Rather, it is
to allow teachers more time to fully cover the kindergarten
curriculum and children more time to discover and experience the wondrous activities that will make their first year of
school so exciting.

Our Daily Schedule

7:55–8:20	Math tubs (manipulatives) and small group math lessons
8:20–8:35	Class meeting/restroom and drinks
8:35–8:55	Math board/calendar
8:55–9:10	Whole class math lesson
9:10–9:20	Predictable chart

9:20–9:50	Shared reading (big books/poem and song charts)
9:50–10:15	Learning centers
10:15–10:30	Morning recess
10:30–10:55	Learning centers continue
10:55–11:10	Alphabet/phonics lesson
11:10–11:40	Writing workshop (journals) or Rainbow Reading Lab (sequenced file folder activities). The Title 1 teacher is in my room at this time.
11:40–12:20	Lunch and recess
12:20–1:10	Special classes (music, counseling, PE, art, or computers)
1:10–1:45	Nap/rest time
1:45–2:00	Afternoon recess
2:00–2:15	Picture and word chart
2:15–3:00	Theme-related activities integrating science and/or social studies
3:00–3:10	"Show and Tell" and get ready to go home

The Effect of Full-Day Kindergarten

Dianne Rothenberg is associate director of the ERIC Clearinghouse on Elementary and Early Childhood Education and founder of PARENTS AskERIC and the National Parent Information Network. She has also written a number of journal articles, book chapters, and conference papers on early childhood education.

Full-day kindergarten was perfect for my two oldest children and awful for my youngest son. He was much more clingy and it was just too long a day. Since kindergarten is not mandatory in our state, I am keeping him in preschool for an additional year.

Huong Lan,
mother of Sam, 5,
Hue, 8, and
Y Lan, 12

Increases in the number of single-parent and dual-employment households and the fact that most children spend a large part of the day away from home signal significant changes in American family life compared to a generation ago. These changes in American society and in education over the last twenty years have contributed to the popularity of all-day, every-day kindergarten programs in many communities. Studies show that parents favor a full-day program that reduces the number of transitions kindergartners experience in a typical day.

Researchers have found a broad range of effects of full-day kindergarten, including a positive relationship between participation in full-day kindergarten and later school performance. After comparing similar half-day and full-day programs in a statewide longitudinal study, they found that full-day kindergartners exhibited more independent learning, classroom involvement, productivity in work with peers, and reflectiveness than half-day kindergartners. They were also more likely to approach the teacher and to express less withdrawal, anger, shyness, and blaming behavior than half-day kindergartners. In general, children in full-day programs exhibited more positive behaviors than did pupils in half-day or alternate-days programs.

Research supports the effectiveness of full-day kindergarten programs that are developmentally appropriate, indicating that they have academic and behavioral benefits for young children. In full-day programs, less hectic instruction geared to student needs and appropriate assessment of student progress contributes to the effectiveness of the program. While these can also be characteristics of high-quality half-day programs, many children seem to benefit academically and behaviorally from all-day kindergarten. Of course, the length of the school day is only one dimension of the kindergarten experience. Other important issues include the nature of the kindergarten curriculum and the quality of teaching.

Discipline

If patience is a virtue, then the best kindergarten teachers should be considered saints. Having visited a number of classrooms, it is clear that the current philosophy is to use positive reinforcement for good behavior rather than criticizing naughtiness.

A typical example was Mrs. Woo's class at a private school. The children had spent the last half-hour working on their Father's Day books. At the end of the period, Mrs. Woo asked them all to stop, put away their markers, clean their desks, place their books on a specifically designated table, and join the class circle on the carpet for story time.

There was a bustle of activity, and it initially seemed as if everyone was complying with the teacher's directive. As each child finished some part of the task, Mrs. Woo would say, "Look at how well Nicole is listening and cleaning her desk. I see that Jason, Skylar, Michelle, and Hunter are doing a good job putting away their markers. Christopher is already sitting in the circle. Good job, Christopher."

Of course, the compliments are a way of modeling good behavior and an impetus for all the children who thrive on affirmation to comply. But the subtlety of this approach seemed to escape the rapscallions.

As a classroom volunteer, I wouldn't say that her teacher was too strict; she was just erratic. I chalked it up to inexperience.

Rachel, mother of
Jessica, 7

At that time there were thirty children in our daughter's kindergarten class, three of whom were major disciplinary problems. I was just amazed at how well the teacher handled everyone. While I don't believe in spanking children, there was one kid I would have liked to throw out the window.

Tina, mother of
Dylan, 8 months,
and Jessica, 6

Peter took this opportunity to squeeze glue on the table. Jared left his mess where it was and gleefully joined circle time. Amanda clandestinely continued applying black marker to her fingernails. Somewhat surprised by the overt defiance of these three adorable children, I wondered how the teacher would handle it.

As Mrs. Woo quickly surveyed the room, Jared was the easiest offender to identify. "Jared," she said calmly, "have you forgotten something?"

"No," he quietly replied with his head bowed down.

"It looks like all your supplies are still on your desk."

"Oh," he said as if taken by surprise.

"I think you need to leave our circle, go back to your desk, and put everything away. Can you please do that?"

Jared, obviously a neophyte at deception, nodded, quickly got up, cleaned his desk, and returned to his space in a few minutes' time.

"Good job, Jared," Mrs. Woo said.

Jared smiled.

Peter also was a pushover. The teacher's aide had evidently told him to get a sponge and paper towels and wash and dry the desk. He accomplished his task with dispatch and joined the circle.

But Amanda was hard-core. She defied the aide who had asked her to wash her hands. She ignored Mrs. Woo's suggestion to listen to the aide. It was truly a standoff. I breathlessly waited to see what would happen. There was absolute silence in the room as the teacher put down the book she had begun reading, got up from her rocking chair, and walked toward Amanda, who didn't blanch.

Within moments, as if choreographed, the aide sat in the teacher's chair and continued reading the story. Mrs. Woo led Amanda to the back of the room, where they had a private conversation. The next thing I saw was Amanda at the sink washing her hands while Mrs. Woo helped scrub her nails. Task accomplished, Mrs. Woo relieved the aide, and with Amanda sitting on her lap, continued reading.

Mystified by the resolution of this conflict, I whispered to the aide, "What did Mrs. Woo say?"

"With Amanda," the aide answered, "it's just a question of defining boundaries and setting consequences. She wants to make sure you won't cave in, and then she'll usually do what you ask. It's very important for her to know you still love her despite her behavior."

Awed by the complexity of the situation, the teacher's seamless method of handling it, and the forbearance it must take to respond so patiently day after day, my eyes filled with tears.

Discipline for Self-Control

Adapted from *Helping Children Learn Self-Control* by the National Association for the Education of Young Children.

Ask any parent or teacher what is most difficult about raising children and the answer will be discipline. Broken rules, tantrums, lack of cooperation—all are real problems for parents and teachers.

We want to stop children from doing whatever it is we don't like or we know is harmful. So when children misbehave, we get frustrated. But does punishment help children build self-control? Do they learn how to cope with strong feelings and tough problems if they are punished?

The answer is a resounding "No!" When children are *punished*, their behavior is controlled through fear. Their feelings are not respected. They behave only to avoid a penalty or to get a bribe. And the adult tells the child only what *not* to do. Children who are punished feel humiliated, hide their mistakes, tend to be angry and aggressive, and fail to develop control of themselves.

When children are *disciplined*, they are shown positive alternatives rather than just told "no." They are taught to see how their actions affect others. Good behavior is rewarded. Adults establish fair, simple rules and consistently enforce

*W*hen I was in kindergarten, my friends and I knew when we had done something wrong because of our teacher's reaction. As I was putting my son to bed one night, he said he thought *he'd been bad* at school that day. "Why?" I asked. "My teacher told me to keep my feet on the ground," he said. "What did you do?" I asked him. "I kicked Sam," he said, and fell asleep.

Harry, father of Max, 4, and Josh, 6

My daughter's teacher was a "screamer" and my daughter was scared to death of her. We parents were afraid to say anything because we weren't sure what the consequences would be for our children.

Carolyn, mother of
Eileen, 3, and
Corby, 7

them. Children who are disciplined learn to share and co-operate. They are better able to handle their anger. They are more self-disciplined and feel successful and in control of themselves.

Guidelines for Classroom Discipline

Lawrence Balzer, Ph.D., a child psychologist, is a professor of applied psychology at New York University. He is the author of *Child Psychology: A Handbook of Contemporary Issues.*

Concepts of Discipline

- Teach children routines and how to follow instructions.
- Guide them in appropriate interactions with one another.
- Encourage self-discipline through guidance, example, and skill development.

Common Problems

- Separation from family
- Making new friends
- Anxiety that accompanies acquisition of new knowledge
- Learning of new routines
- Adjusting to a new environment

Effective Resolutions

- Children need to be informed about their teachers' expectations.

- They should be shown how to perform their tasks.

- They need to be corrected as they attempt their duties.

- They should be offered encouragement for their effort.

- They should receive recognition for their achievements.

- Expectations should be high but in accordance with their age and developmental level.

- Occasional loss of privileges might serve as a deterrent to unwanted activities.

Parental Role

- Parents should be invited to class on a regular basis.

- They should be encouraged to volunteer for class trips and various school activities.

- They should be kept informed about children's status on a regular basis.

One Teacher's Plan

Amy Griffith has been a kindergarten teacher for eleven years. She teaches at Crewe Primary School in Crewe, Virginia.

I base our classroom discipline plan on our school's discipline policy. Mine is a visual approach: a beehive and bees. When parents visit the classroom, they always ask, "What does it mean to get your bee moved?" I explain that each child has a bee with his or her name on it. All the bees are put on the beehive. Beside the beehive are colors representing the consequences of specific behavioral problems. Yellow is a warning. Blue is a time-out. Green means the child misses five minutes of playtime. Orange represents a note home. Red is a visit to the principal.

I thought I had patience until I saw my child's kindergarten teacher. Watching her discipline the children was more helpful than any parenting book I've ever read.

Mary Lou, mother of Brad, 1, Barbara, 5, and Becky, 6

When children do something inappropriate, they have to move their bee out of the beehive to yellow, and so on. At the end of the day, if a child's bee is still in the beehive she gets a sticker on the behavior chart. A child who doesn't get her bee moved all week becomes an "All Star" for the week, gets a special treat, and her name is posted in the hallway.

First-Day Jitters

N o one ever told me that starting kindergarten would be so difficult—for me. The night before school began, Alex was cautiously excited. After he went to bed I threw up.

"I think you're overreacting," Bernie sensibly said.

"Easy for you to say," I shrugged. "You get to go to work. I'm the one who's taking him to the orientation."

"He'll be fine," Bernie calmly replied. "Look at how well he adjusted to preschool. I don't think he experienced a moment of separation anxiety."

"Are you kidding?" I shrieked. "He and I visited the school three times together before I left him. For a month when I dropped him off, I spent ten minutes every morning waving good-bye from the parking lot. It wasn't that easy," I reminded him.

"He's been going to the elementary school summer program two days a week for the last six weeks just to get used to the school," Bernie countered.

"That's different," I said harshly. "There were relatively few kids. During the school year there are 32 children in four different kindergarten classes—which means there will be 128

When my daughter started kinder-garten, I was embarrassed that she adjusted more easily than I. She waved good-bye and didn't look back. I immediately developed a severe case of empty nest syndrome.

Moji, mother of Jordan, 5, and Habib, 7

69

Having been a kindergarten teacher for many years, I know that it's not a good idea to focus too much on the first day. It makes separation anxiety so much harder. So you can imagine my surprise when our daughter started kindergarten, and the moment we started walking toward school, my husband took our video camera from the trunk of our car, began making funny faces so that she would smile, and recorded the entire experience.

Loretta, mother of
Marianne, 6

children and their parents that first day," I said before bolting into the bathroom a second time.

When I reappeared, Bernie solicitously asked, "Honey, do you want me to take the time off from work and go with you?"

"That's not necessary," I replied somewhat forlornly. I knew he had a pressing deadline. "We'll manage," I added, putting a cold compress on my forehead because I had a splitting headache. Although I awoke several times during the night in a sweat, both Bernie and Alex slept peacefully.

The next morning, even though I was fraught with apprehension, I was a surprisingly calm role model for Alex. As we drove to school and he asked me what I remembered about my own first day of kindergarten, I was positive without being rah-rah; informative without overdoing it. (Okay, if the truth be known, I have actually no idea what my first day of kindergarten was like, and my mother has blocked it out. So I pretended I remembered and he liked the story.)

Once Alex and I got to school, everything was fine. The orientation was a wonderful way to make the transition. I was relieved to find that other parents were as nervous as I was. (Either that or collectively we are a tense group of people whose faces are usually pinched with anxiety and we tend to sigh often and loudly.)

The principal was great in allaying our fears. She was warm, witty, and well organized. The teachers seemed gentle and caring. All in all, it was a terrific beginning. Alex took it in stride and confidently waved when we parents left our children with their new teachers for a half-hour.

Later, when I called Bernie at work to tell him the good news, he sounded awful. He said he'd been a nervous wreck all morning and that he'd been taking an antacid nonstop. Clearly my anxiety had been channeled to him.

When he asked how things had gone, I wasn't sure how to respond. "It was emotionally draining but manageable," I mumbled. "Alex was a real trooper; I think he had a good time."

There was an anticipatory pause. "Okay, so I overreacted a bit," I admitted. "You were right."

We both started laughing with relief as if to acknowledge that we'd survived yet another milestone of Alex's development with our marriage intact. "Thank God for small favors."

Easing the Transition

Patty Kranker, from Westwood Charter Elementary School in Los Angeles, has taught kindergarten for seven years.

During the first day of kindergarten, which we refer to as Separation Day, the children spend an hour in the classroom with me while their parents are in the auditorium with our principal. When the children and I are first alone, I point to the clock and explain to them that their parents will be back to pick them up when the big hand is on the twelve and the little hand is on the eleven. Then I take roll. When the children hear their names, they walk to the front of the class, and I give them name tags.

After we're done with the roll, the children sit on a rug in front of my chair, and I read them *Franklin Goes to School* by Paulette Bourgeois and Brenda Clark. What's nice about this story is that when Franklin, the tortoise, goes to kindergarten for the first day, he exhibits many of the same feelings and has many of the same experiences that all kindergartners do. He awakens early but he's too nervous to eat much breakfast. It takes him a long time to hug his parents good-bye. He worries whether he'll be ready for school because he cannot write like his friend Rabbit or read like his friend Beaver. But his teacher, Mr. Owl, is warm and nurturing, and Franklin has a very good day.

After I finish the story, I say, "On the first day of school, we have many feelings. Some of us are happy. Others are sad. Some are nervous, and some of us don't know how we feel."

Our older son's entire kindergarten experience was traumatic for us. My wife and I both dropped him off that first morning, stayed and listened to the principal's speech, watched him go to class with his teacher, and brought him home. He wanted a play date with a neighborhood child. We flipped a coin to determine who had to stay awake to supervise it. We were both ready to go to bed and it was only eleven o'clock in the morning.

Terese, mother of Joshua, 7, and Stuart, 8

I'm a lawyer and a single mom, and on the first day of school I was in the midst of a court case. I dropped my daughter off at school, told her teacher that my nanny would pick her up, and three years later, I still remember her plaintive cry, "Mommmmy," across the school yard.

Greta, mother of
Hannah, 15

I continue with questions like, "How do you think Franklin feels? How do you feel?"

I show the children a "feeling graph" I have placed on the wall. There are four columns with the words "happy," "sad," "nervous," and "I don't know." Above the words are faces which represent these feelings. When children share their feelings, they put a Post-It with their name on the graph under the picture of the face that best describes their feelings. Once we're done, I explain that feelings change. "The graph will still be up tomorrow, and some of us may feel differently than we do today," I say. "If we do, we can move the Post-It with our name and place it under another feeling."

Just as I promised, when the big hand is on the twelve and the little hand is on the eleven, the parents come to pick up their children. I briefly talk, then give them an information packet of material introducing me and my class aide, detailing our daily schedule and explaining the classroom rules. We recommend that parents separate food for recess and for lunchtime and suggest that the children bring everything to school in a backpack. If a child is having a difficult adjustment period, I suggest the parent include a favorite stuffed animal or a family picture.

Before everyone goes home, I talk about what to expect the next day, which is the first full day of kindergarten. I explain that the children will line up right outside our classroom door. I suggest that each parent and child agree on a ritual for saying good-bye (whether it's two kisses and a hug or one big kiss), so that after the good-byes, the child understands that his or her parent will leave. What is important for parents to realize is that there is a reason for ritualizing our good-byes. Otherwise, the children don't know what to expect, particularly if their parents peek through a window or linger outside after saying good-bye. And that concludes the first day.

The second day is a bigger adjustment. We begin school at 8:20 A.M. and end at 1:30 P.M. This is the day when we begin learning our school routine. When the children arrive,

I show them where to put their backpacks and their lunch tickets (if they will be eating in the cafeteria). We talk about school safety. We take a tour of the school and meet the principal and the people who work in the office. And then we slowly ease into our routine. It is the first real day of separation and the beginning of the "bonding" period between the children and me. The more quickly they learn that I am a safe person and school is a safe place, the easier it will be to adjust.

At the end of this day, the children who attend the after-school program will be picked up at the classroom. The children remaining in the room will be picked up by their parents, hopefully on time. Again, this is part of the ritual. It is important for children to know that when school is over, their parents will be waiting for them.

For some children, the transition to kindergarten will take three days to a week. For others, it will be longer. But all parents should rest assured that ultimately, unless there is a special problem, your child will adjust to kindergarten. And so will you.

Friends

A.J. was very shy. After a month of kindergarten, he didn't seem to have made any new friends. I was concerned and talked to his teacher. She told me the names of the children he played with in class. I arranged play dates, and suddenly he had three best friends.

Linda, mother of
Devon, 6, and
A.J., 9

"My daughter, Devon, was somewhat of a loner in preschool," her father, Larry, a single parent, said. "There were a few boys she played with, mostly in the sandbox. But her best friend was Jordan. The girls were inseparable, and Devon was totally content. Jordan's family lives down the block from us and the girls played together almost every day.

"Perhaps I should have foreseen a problem down the road because Jordan is more outgoing than Devon and always has had many other friends. It's never been a problem because Devon likes to play more on her own than Jordan does. She loves Legos, she looks at picture books and works on puzzles. She's got this great dollhouse, and she and I do sports together.

"For the first few weeks of kindergarten, everything was fine. But after the transition period, Jordan began having play dates with other girls. When she arrived at school one day and announced to Devon that Melanie was her new best friend, Devon was crushed. She came home in tears.

"That afternoon Devon and I had a long talk about friendship, how people change, and what that can do to relationships. I assured her that Jordan would still be her friend

74

and maybe even her best friend again. But I also said that maybe we'd both learned a lesson from this experience; that it was time to branch out. Devon wasn't convinced this was a good idea, but I told her I would talk to her teacher, Mr. Randall, whom she already liked a lot.

"That evening when Devon was asleep I called Jordan's mother, Marie, and told her what had happened. She felt terrible that Jordan had been so hurtful. Marie said she would talk to Jordan about the way to treat friends, but we agreed that we wouldn't push the girls together.

"The next afternoon I met with Mr. Randall and explained the situation. He was great, very sympathetic. He recognized that Devon was shy in groups, that she was much better in one-on-one situations, and that she tended to observe for a while rather than participate. On the other hand, she was a leader on the playground. I had known all of this from preschool.

"What was new was that Mr. Randall suggested that he would help Devon work on extending her social skills and that I would reinforce it at home. We discussed ways to help Devon feel more comfortable in group situations, to be more outgoing in joining other kids in activities, and to learn how to respond to overtures from other children. Mr. Randall identified a few girls whose interests and personalities seemed similar to Devon's. I called the moms and arranged for play dates. There was no immediate match, but at least Devon was feeling more comfortable at school. By now, Jordan had returned to the fold, but Devon was distrustful of her.

"Anyway, it turned out to be a great year for Devon. She loves building blocks and this other little girl, Zoe, does too. After a month or so, Zoe became Devon's fast friend.

"Zoe lives about twenty minutes away and she's the youngest of five children. Her parents are very low-key but the household bustles with activity. They've got rabbits, cats, a dog, and gerbils. There's a great climbing structure in the backyard, and there are always kids around. It's been a terrific experience for Devon, and she's grown in many ways.

"Zoe likes coming to our house as well. One day she said to me, 'You know, Larry, I love being here. It's so quiet and I don't have to share.'

"I bit my lip to keep from laughing aloud. I'd grown up in a large family myself and could totally relate to the feeling."

The Art of Making Friends

Lilian Katz is the director of the ERIC Clearinghouse on Elementary and Early Childhood Education and professor emerita at the University of Illinois at Urbana-Champaign.

My oldest son and youngest daughter easily made friends. In kindergarten, my daughter wanted so many play dates that I had to apply limits. I'm not that social and had begun feeling like my home was a child-care center.

Michelle, mother of Leslie, 6, Asher, 8, Karen, 9, and Harry, 11

Though the art of making friends seems to come naturally to most children, it requires a good deal of experience and usually involves lots of trial and error. Observations of children successful in making friends indicate that they use such skills as giving appropriate responses to their own actions or the actions of others, like "excuse me" or "thanks a lot." They also make positive suggestions to others, offer to help and to contribute to the activities of others, use phrases that encourage an exchange of information such as "you know what?," and readily respond in turn with "No! What?" They are likely to express their desires clearly to request information from others about their intentions and wishes, to refrain from calling attention to themselves, and to enter ongoing interests by exploring ways in which they are similar to other children: likes, experiences, or characteristics they and their peers have in common.

THE PARENTS' ROLE

Recent research suggests that parents have an important role in helping develop and refine their children's friendship-making skills. As it is in many other aspects of children's development, having warm, supportive, and encouraging parents to whom the child feels deeply, securely, and affectionately attached seems to be basic to the development of social competence. Not surprisingly, there is ample reason to believe that parents' own reactions with their friends provide the young child with models and clues about the skills involved.

PROVIDE LOTS OF OPPORTUNITIES

Some activities are more conducive to the development of social skills than others—a youngster is far more likely to be in a position to test his or her social skills at the neighborhood playground than at home with a box full of toys. Opportunities for spontaneous, unstructured play among young children under the supervision of a knowledgeable adult are essential. Many children who have difficulty making friends become excluded from social activities, and thus have less experience and fewer opportunities to develop, learn, practice, and refine the skills they lack. It takes seven or eight years to develop and refine the wide range of skills required for making and keeping friends. Thus it is a good idea to start early in providing a child with lots of warmth and support, and with frequent opportunities to make and keep friends.

A Lesson in Friendship

Janelle Luckett teaches kindergarten at Arcola Elementary School in Arcola, Indiana.

Part of the excitement about starting kindergarten is the opportunity to make new friends. It seems to come more naturally for young children than it does for adults. Children are not usually as critical or judgmental of their peers.

In kindergarten, we teach friendship from day one. Before our students enter the classroom, we try to create a physical environment with the goal of enhancing friendship;

Our older son has never had difficulties making friends, although I would say that we initially helped him develop the necessary skills. Our younger son is much more of a loner. He likes being by himself, although his teacher felt he needed extra socialization. She recommended I set up a play date with a child with similar interests and he now has a best friend.

Tomiko, mother of
Alec, 6, and
David, 10

a nonthreatening place where children feel safe and comfortable. Part of my method of teaching children how to relate to each other is what I call the *five lifelong guidelines*:

1. Do not use put-downs.

2. Do your personal best.

3. Practice active listening.

4. Be truthful.

5. Be trustworthy.

During community circle, we discuss these guidelines. Children also learn through role modeling and daily interactions with other kindergartners. I encourage children to follow this practice at home as well as at school. By applying this behavior to real-life situations, the children begin to understand the importance of friendships.

Making and keeping friends requires the ability to learn how to work on and solve problems as they arise. As in any friendship, there are bound to be disagreements. The children are taught a process that is called the "debug" system to work out problems. They can ignore the behavior they don't like. They can ask the person politely to "please stop." They can move away. They can use "I" statements to tell the person what bothers them. They can get adult help. When children use these steps, they can solve problems, gain a sense of independence, and develop the necessary skills to maintain friendships.

Gender

‑ ‑

At a meeting with a group of kindergarten moms, it became clear once again that there's a huge difference between girls and boys.

"My son David hasn't received a happygram [a note for good behavior] all year," Lorraine complained. "If it's not one thing, it's another. He doesn't pay attention at story time, he's not cooperative lining up, and he doesn't cut well."

Everyone laughed.

"I'm serious. Do you know how many things the children must cut each day? I talked with a friend who's a teacher. She said not to worry about it because boys' fine motor skills are not as advanced as girls'. Anyway, I'm reconciled to the fact that David's not going to be a brain surgeon when he grows up."

Again, there was laughter.

"I just don't think teachers handle boys as well," replied Cheryl, the mother of a kindergartner and a first-grader. "Ariel's teacher loved her because she was cooperative, polite, and a good listener. Ariel participated in the morning calendar meeting. She followed directions and she loved to hug her teacher. But Andrew is another story. The only things he's interested in doing at school are building blocks and playing.

My son definitely had a difficult time sitting quietly on the floor during circle time. My wife was concerned; I wasn't. Somehow I didn't think that floor sitting was an important skill.

Jim, father of
Barry, 8

I believe teachers have greater expectations that girls will behave more quietly. Most did, except our daughter, Sequoia. She's got three older brothers. The teacher would call me to complain about her behavior at least one or two days a week for the first month. I finally asked for a parent conference. I told her that the boys' mothers I had talked to said that their sons, who were exhibiting similar behavior, were not getting phone calls. I told her that my husband and I didn't believe in gender stereotyping. The phone calls stopped the next day.

Cindy, mother of Sequoia, 6, Normandy, 9, Denver, 11, and Adan, 13

Last week he ate the macaroni he was supposed to use to make a necklace. When I asked him why, he said he was hungry," she said ruefully.

"It all comes down to gender," Darvina, a mother of four, suggested. "My girls have always done better in school than my boys. They're more socially adept and more accommodating."

"Let's face it!" Margo interjected. "You've all taught your daughters to be suck-ups." Everyone laughed before Margo continued. "No kid is naturally polite. Sharing is a learned skill, just like sitting on the floor in a circle and listening. I feel proud that Lily is independent, high-spirited, and self-expressive."

"The point is," said Mia, the mother of Evie and Ryan, "elementary school is designed for girls. There are mostly women teachers and women principals. There is an emphasis on the cerebral, not the physical. When I volunteer in the classroom, boys are reprimanded much more often than girls, except for Lily, who I'm convinced will either lead a motorcycle gang or be the first woman president of the United States."

Once all the moms had left my house to pick up their kindergartners, I drove to school because it was lunchtime and I'd forgotten to put Alex's sandwich in his lunch bag. He was sitting on the bench next to his best friend, Max. I gave Alex the sandwich. He said Max had already shared his.

"Why are you guys sitting on the bench?" I asked as I plopped down next to them.

"Mrs. Margolis saw me hit Max," Alex said.

"I hit him first," Max forthrightly disclosed. "We were just playing around."

"Were you benched too?" I asked Max.

"Nah, Alex didn't tell on me. Ya know, Susan, they just don't like boys here."

"Is that so?" I asked.

"Yeah," Alex said. "The girls sit quietly together, say bad things to each other, and one of them always runs away crying. No one ever gets punished."

"We sock each other and we're benched right away," Max said. "It's not fair."

I didn't know what to say; I thought they were probably right. So I patted them both on the head and walked to my car thinking, "Boys will be boys, and that's really okay."

Girls and Boys

Beth A. Haines, Ph.D., a developmental psychologist, is an associate professor of psychology and a member of the Gender Studies Program at Lawrence University in Appleton, Wisconsin.

What are the differences between kindergarten boys and girls in terms of learning styles, socialization, teacher-pupil relationships, and motor development?

Although there is substantial variation among children in all the characteristics noted above, these differences are *not* gender related. That is, there is greater variation within each gender (girls to girls, boys to boys), for example in social skills, learning styles, and cognitive skills, than there is between the genders.

Still, there are a few reliable gender differences that are apparent in kindergarten-age children. Young girls typically show superior vocabulary, reading comprehension, and verbal creativity (although this difference is not apparent in later development). Boys are more likely to engage in physical aggression or be the victims of it, whereas girls are more likely to use indirect aggression such as excluding a child from a social activity. Dependent upon parent and teacher response, some of these differences are likely to arise or be magnified. If aggressive children are disciplined, that behavior is likely to decrease in frequency. If social exclusion is discussed and dealt with, it too is less likely to continue.

Of course, among all children, there are also individual differences. Some girls tend to be more aggressive (usually considered a male trait) and some boys are more sensitive and emotional (usually considered a female trait). Yet, boys and girls are equally social and good at rote learning. They have comparable levels of self-esteem. People who work in gender studies argue that treating stereotypes as real differences can be harmful to children. Consequently, the happy, well-adjusted child who enjoys activities that are not consistent with stereotypes of his or her gender may become unhappy, solely because of social feedback.

Obviously, this is a controversial area as there are also substantial differences among parents and among cultures in the extent to which they teach and endorse stereotypical behavior. However, one interesting finding is that three- to six-year-old children are more conscious of gender stereotypes than adults. The reason is that young children tend to take rules literally and believe they should be rigidly followed. Many times when children go to toy stores and see pink aisles with dolls and art supplies, and blue aisles with sports equipment and action figures, they typically go to the aisle that is clearly intended for them.

Some parents (consciously or not) expect their children to follow gender conventions. In particular, many parents are more comfortable when their girls play with male-stereotyped toys than when their boys play with female-stereotyped toys.

As a parent who tried to model behavior by interest rather than by gender, I was glad to see that in kindergarten the children didn't segregate each other by sex. By third grade, I was appalled when they voluntarily did.

Cary, mother of
Gracie, 6, and
Ivy, 8

How should kindergarten teachers deal with gender issues?

Research suggests that teachers may unintentionally respond to boys and girls differently. When boys struggle in academic areas, teachers sometimes feel it is because they are unwilling to work or disinterested in what is being taught. This is seen as behavior that can be easily modified. Because girls are often more compliant than boys, they usually are more successful in school. So when girls struggle academically, it is sometimes attributed to a lack of ability, which in our culture is seen as more difficult to modify. Thus, girls and boys may get different messages about their ability to succeed in academics, especially in gender-stereotyped areas.

It is important for teachers to break down these stereotypes. Some girls excel in math and science (typically considered male-dominant fields) and some boys excel in art and music (typically considered female-dominant fields). If teachers avoid stereotypic expectations, children will be better able to pursue their interests without the restrictions imposed by gender stereotypes.

Teachers should also model a broader acceptance of a range of behavior and be careful not to label activities as most appropriate for girls or boys. Both parents and teachers should know that kindergartners are wonderful learners and are powerfully affected by the adults in their lives. They have fewer preconceived notions of what is "normal" and what is not, and kindergarten is an ideal place to model gender and racial equality and harmony.

Gifted Children

In second grade, my daughter and son tested as gifted. In kindergarten, they seemed average to us.

Catherine, mother
of Greg and
Sissy, both 8

"Alex, do you care if I write an essay on your being gifted?" I asked my son.

"Yeah," he answered.

So I decided to write the story my friend Marty told me about his daughter Emma.

"A month after Emma started kindergarten, I was amazed when one day at lunch a law associate asked me if Emma was gifted.

"'Gifted?' I asked. 'How can I tell? She doesn't know how to write her name.'

"'Oh,' they all nodded.

"'Oh, what?'

"'Eric taught himself to read at three,' Colin said.

"'When Katrina entered kindergarten, she could count to fifty,' her father Richard bragged.

"Before he realized how ridiculous the conversation was, even my best friend Ted said, 'Oliver knew his ABCs in preschool.'

"'You're comparing the intelligence level of elementary school kids?' I asked in amazement. 'This is not billable hours, guys. Neither is it a competition.' Completely annoyed, I walked away from the table.

"That night at home, when Emma was asleep, I asked my wife, Lilly, whether Emma was gifted.

" 'Gifted?' she scoffed, with disdain. 'Honestly, Marty. Do you think you could wait a few years until they determine that in school?'

" 'It's not me,' I responded. She raised her eyebrows. 'It was Colin, Richard, and Ted.'

" 'What can you expect from Colin and Richard? They're jerks. They compare everything from their cars to their trophy wives. But Ted?' she asked, with disappointment. 'Rebecca [Ted's wife and Lilly are good friends] would be furious if she knew he was participating in this inane discussion.'

" 'I just wondered,' I said, backing off.

" 'If you must know,' Lilly explained, 'at our school they test children at the end of second grade who have been recommended by their teachers. I'm not sure of the criteria, but I've heard they classify them as highly gifted, gifted, or normal. It won't mean anything for Emma because our school has no special program for the gifted; they integrate the children in regular classrooms. It only matters in middle school because we could then apply for a gifted magnet school.'

" 'How do you know so much about this?' I asked.

" 'Because last year Cassie told me that Brian was tested, and she explained everything. The funny part was that Cassie forgot she had signed the permission slip for the test. Then one day out of the blue, a school psychologist called to say Brian was highly gifted. Since Cassie hadn't expected the call, she was so taken aback that all she said was thank you and hung up. Later she figured that the woman must have thought she was a moron because she had no questions.'

" 'What can you expect?' I asked. 'Cassie is an actress.' Lilly threw a pillow at me.

"That night I dreamed about Emma. If she was gifted, I wondered whether she should attend a special school. I worried she would be bored in a public school. I pictured my beautiful little girl as a college student who was wearing black-

When I volunteered in my son's classroom, I was awed by the children who already knew how to read. One kid's vocabulary seemed to be better than my own.

Lyn, mother of
Christopher, 6

rimmed glasses with a tape wrapped around the nose bridge. I was exhausted by the time I awakened.

"When the alarm rang, I told Lilly about my dreams and seriously asked her what we would do if Emma were gifted.

"'We would love her the same way we would if she's not.'

"That's why I'm crazy about Lilly," Marty said. "She always reminds me what is important."

Meeting Gifted Children's Needs

Pamela Pearson, a former kindergarten teacher, is the coordinator-teacher for the gifted program in District 206 in Alexandria, Minnesota.

When providing services for kindergarten-age gifted children, the most important component is flexibility. These children, while usually verbally precocious and more advanced in analytical thinking than their age peers, often exhibit an uneven developmental pattern. For example, they may be able to read at a sixth-grade level yet be significantly below their peers in small motor control and therefore have difficulty holding a pencil or writing their name. In structuring one program to fit the needs of every student at this level, teachers must accommodate individual needs and interests with a flexible curriculum and delivery method. Consequently, the program should be readily adaptable to the individual children involved, providing opportunities to go beyond the established kindergarten curriculum. The program also needs to be inclusive enough to meet their social and behavioral needs.

In regard to the effectiveness of pull-out programs, research clearly indicates that gifted children should spend at least *some* time during their school day with children of similar ability in order to thrive academically. Many gifted children anxiously await the start of kindergarten only to discover they already know everything that is being covered by the teacher in class. This causes some children to react with passivity, waiting patiently for something new, while others turn off to education (though not to learning) and become underachievers. Still others become behavior problems, using self-stimulation to keep themselves interested in their surroundings. Except in large metropolitan areas where options are more readily available, full-time special classes may not be an option. In some rural areas where this isn't an option we try to provide opportunities for these children to learn something new and exciting every day through flexible grouping and individual challenges. This may mean an advanced curriculum with fellow students in the primary grades or delving into a special research topic from the kindergarten curriculum. Precocious math students have found challenge in thinking games, math manipulatives, and computers. In extreme cases, students have combined grade levels, completing kindergarten and first grade in one school year. The method must vary based on the skills, personality, and ability level of the child, but these children are entitled to an education commensurate with their needs.

> *We didn't know our son was gifted; we just knew he was bored.*
>
> Val, father of Brian, 9

Gifted Programs

Joseph S. Renzulli, Ed.D., is the director of The National Research Center on the Gifted and Talented at the University of Connecticut.

How do you determine if your kindergarten child is gifted?

That question is one of the most difficult to deal with because I am against labeling a child, especially at an early age. What I prefer is using a behavioral definition that addresses a child's talents and strengths without labeling him or her "gifted." We encourage and support the child's particular abilities rather than lumping children into one homogenous category.

We look for behaviors that are not typical of other agemates, such as a child who has learned to read with little or no assistance, or a child who understands numerical relationships beyond what other kids his or her age may know. There are kindergartners who can name three or four different ways to put coins together to make twenty-five cents, whereas most kids might only know that twenty-five cents is a quarter or that two nickels are a dime. A remarkable memory for detail is another quality to look for. If you ask one of these children about a movie, he or she can retell it frame by frame. They can vividly describe a place they have been or remember every detail of a story. I have seen kindergartners grasp all these concepts, although this kind of ability usually doesn't become evident until two or three years later.

Schools provide a lot of services for the special needs children. It doesn't seem fair that the gifted children get short shrift.

Shelee, mother of Daren, 8, and Maggie, 12

Another sign of a more advanced child is one who is sensitive to his or her surroundings. This child might see humor in situations that other children do not. Such children are interested and ask questions about cause-effect relationships. "What would happen if? How come? Why did so and so do that?" They seem to be interested in more abstract concepts, such as fairness. I have seen bright young kids who have a greater sensitivity to issues of fairness, right or wrong, and good or bad. Some of these children express themselves through art. They can draw a picture and tell a wonderful story about it. Other kids speak, write, or do math well. Some children are quite clever at constructing things, such as Lego blocks and building sets. There is a wide variety of talents that parents can look for, support, and encourage.

A huge range in abilities exists within an average kindergarten class. Some of this disparity has to do with preschool experience, but some children do have remarkable skills and talents that need to be nurtured and supported.

What can parents of gifted children expect from their local elementary schools?

Some schools obviously do a good job and some do not. Making accommodations for a child in specific areas of advanced development is important. If a child is reading, he or she will not be interested in learning a letter a week. Schools should have an enrichment specialist on hand to help keep those kids engaged. Enrichment specialists are defined in various ways in various school districts but are basically people who have some background, experience, and training in modifying the regular curriculum to provide more challenge for bright kids.

Each school needs to look at the strengths of each child. We use a Total Talent Portfolio, where we document children's strengths, not just in traditional academic areas, but in learning styles and expression styles. If I know a five-year-old who is tremendously interested in dinosaurs or boats or airplanes, then I can find high-interest activities that will enhance his reading. If a child is interested in airplanes, get her books on airplanes. What is important is to allow these children to work on more challenging material. If you do, you will not have to fight the motivation battle because it is usually there to start with.

Our school has an excellent gifted program; it just doesn't start in kindergarten. We supplemented our kids' education by taking them to museums and concerts and on field trips.

Terri, mother of Todd, 9, and Miranda, 11

Do you think kindergartens should offer pull-out programs and enrichment activities?

Absolutely. Kindergarten is a time when it is extremely important to provide challenges. If school is incredibly dull, that's when you start turning children off to learning.

What can parents do to get additional help for their kids?

The first goal is to see if there is an enrichment specialist in the school and to determine whether the administrators and teachers are willing to make accommodations based on a child's advanced abilities and interests. In addition, parents can look for community programs. I don't mean taking your child to a museum or an aquarium to look at displays, rather to find interesting community classes and programs. There are theater opportunities for kids. Of course you shouldn't make your child go to the theater if she is interested in electrons. Find a subject your child is interested in and look for ways to enhance that interest.

Another suggestion is to get youngsters together with other children who share similar interests. I don't mean you should form a gifted child group; you can do more damage to children by labeling them. But if you or your child knows other kids who are interested in *Star Wars*, get them together and invent some games, do some artwork, make up some stories, or make a video. Think of it as a playgroup with a mission.

What should you do if your child is bored in kindergarten?

Teachers should take the time to find out why the child is bored. I can turn boredom around in a second by taking one book out of a child's hand and replacing it with another. It's that simple. Higher levels of human performance, productivity, and ability always develop more rapidly and enjoyably when children are interested in what they're doing. Teachers should make appropriate adjustments when a child is bored. If the teacher is not taking the initiative, it is all right for the parent to bring it up as long as it is presented in a "Let's figure out a way that we can put our heads together and solve the problem" fashion.

Obviously, it would not be a good idea to walk in and say, "My child is gifted and you're not challenging him," which is exactly what a lot of what I call the bumper-sticker parents do. They are so obsessed with the fact that they've got a "gifted" child that they turn people off. All of our children are the best gifts we ever get. That is why I argue for a behavioral definition of a child's skills and abilities as opposed to labeling a child "gifted." It also takes away some of the political baggage we put on our kids when we act as if they have an extra golden chromosome. They ain't got nothing 'til they put it to work someplace.

Homeschooling

"Our situation is somewhat unique," Jack said on the telephone. "My two brothers and I, our spouses, and children live on a twenty-acre family farm about forty miles away from a city with a population of 50,000 people. Fifteen years ago my brother Jesse, sister-in-law Ellen, and their kids were the first to move back home and build a house. They began homeschooling Callie, my oldest niece, then five years old, because they felt the local elementary school was mediocre at best.

"Ellen, a nurse by profession, did all the legwork, research-ing state laws, visiting other homeschoolers, and contacting homeschooling organizations. She and my mother, a retired high school teacher, figured out the curriculum as they went along. Mom said it was an arduous but satisfying pursuit and that Ellen was a tenacious worker.

"Eight years ago, when my wife, Deb, our children, Danny, Betsy, and Tim, and I moved back home, our eight nieces and nephews were being homeschooled with seven other children from our valley. Other parents were helping teach.

"Now, Ellen and Mom participate in a peripheral way and I'm one of the full-time parent-teachers. The program has evolved over time. With more experience, we've become bet-

We're very religious and we found neither public nor private schools that suited our needs. Homeschooling has been difficult but we have found a community of people who share our values.

Sandra, mother of
Mary, 5, Mark, 9,
and Gabe, 13

91

Our older children went to public schools. Seven years later, we felt that the schools had deteriorated so much that we homeschooled our youngest daughter. After kindergarten we couldn't stand it any longer. She's much happier now that she's in public school, and so are we.

Deidre, mother of
Chloe, 7, Joel, 15,
and Oliver, 17

ter organized. We group the children by age. The younger ones spend a lot of time playing in- and outdoors, learning farm chores (ours is not a self-supporting farm but we grow food and keep livestock), and making art and music. Once they show an interest, we teach them reading, writing, and arithmetic. We've found that everyone learns at his or her own pace. One or two mornings a week, parents take the children on special field trips so the children's world doesn't become too insular.

"The older kids usually work on academic projects in the morning. Sometimes they work alone, other times in smaller or larger groups. We are able to keep the curriculum fresh and challenging because the adults in our community have a wide range of backgrounds, skills, and interests. Many of the teenagers participate in different programs—music, computer, science, sports—in our town, which, like the entire valley, has grown significantly in the intervening years. They also do volunteer work, or have after-school jobs.

"For a wide variety of reasons, some of our children are never homeschooled and others decide to stop being homeschooled and attend public school. Since kindergarten, our eight-year-old daughter, Betsy, who has multiple learning disabilities, has attended a special education program at an elementary school about twenty miles away. A few of the older kids, including my niece Callie, and son Danny, have enrolled in public middle or high school because they wanted a more 'active' social life or wanted to participate more fully in sports or other school activities.

"As our children and our world have grown, the school has evolved. Some families have left because there were personality conflicts, or they were uncomfortable with the educational or social direction in which we were moving. Because of technological advances, other professionals who can now work at home and live where they'd like have joined the fray. So we have had some wonderful additions to our community."

When I asked Jack to reflect upon his experiences as a homeschooling parent, he E-mailed back. "The freedom to homeschool my children is representative of an entire lifestyle I hadn't envisioned. For eighteen years I was an advertising executive in a large Los Angeles agency. Deb was, and still is, a financial planner; she has an office at home. Our life was fast-paced, and we liked it. When our children were of school age, we were ready to move home. Because we were financially secure, we were able to make that choice.

"We never worried about our children's education—ordinarily a preeminent concern—because the homeschooling framework was in place. Had that not been available, I know I wouldn't have had the wherewithal to undertake a responsibility of such magnitude.

"So how do I sum things up?" he rhetorically wrote. "Deb and I feel inordinately lucky. We live in an idyllic environment. We have a wonderful extended family, and our children are happy. It doesn't get much better than that."

The World as the Classroom

Mary Griffith is the editor of the quarterly *Home-Education Review* and the author of *The Homeschooling Handbook: From Preschool to High School, a Parent's Guide* and *The Unschooling Handbook: How to Use the Whole World as Your Child's Classroom.*

Why do people homeschool their children?

There are as many reasons for homeschooling as there are parents and kids doing it. Some of us discover that we enjoy watching and sharing our preschoolers' learning process and don't see any good reason to let someone else have all that fun just because they suddenly turned school-age. Some families begin homeschooling because of problems with a teacher or administrator, curriculum, peer pressure, or safety concerns. Diagnoses of learning disabilities are often a reason these days as well. Families may disagree with a school diagnosis or treatment plan or determine that learning outside a school setting

Our oldest child attended kindergarten in a large urban school. It was an awful experience for him and for us. During that year, my wife and I read John Holt's How Children Learn, *a seminal book in the field. We spent one year researching all the specifics and E-mailing homeschoolers all over the country and decided to make the commitment. We've never looked back.*

Tom, father of
Tucker, 4, and
Mason, 7

simply suits their child's personality and learning style better. Other families choose homeschooling for religious or philosophical reasons.

How many children in the United States are homeschooled?

Nobody really knows. The problem is that the legal rules for homeschooling vary considerably from state to state, and some states simply have no way of keeping track of the number of homeschoolers within their jurisdiction. Estimates vary, but the most plausible educated guesses put the figure somewhere around 1.5 million children. The one fact we know for sure is that the number is growing.

In homeschooling Ashley, kindergarten was the most difficult year for us. She was interested solely in playing. It was driving us crazy because we were worried about what we would accomplish. When we learned that kindergarten wasn't mandatory in our state, we relaxed. First grade was much better.

Connie, mother of Ashley, 7

What are the advantages and disadvantages of homeschooling?

Oddly enough, the advantages and disadvantages of homeschooling are often exactly the same. Homeschooling puts education directly in the hands of children and parents. While there are plenty of resources for finding help, homeschoolers bear the ultimate responsibility for making it work. Your schedule, your curriculum, your evaluation method are not provided for you—you choose what works with your family and with each individual child. Once you become accustomed to accepting the responsibility, though, it's hard to imagine giving up the flexibility and freedom homeschooling gives our lives.

How does homeschooling affect academic achievement?

It depends entirely on the individual. Homeschooling, to be successful, demands that its practitioners learn how to learn, and most become experts at it. While homeschoolers don't necessarily end up with conventional school transcripts, that unconventionality is certainly no bar to higher education. Homeschoolers generally score at least as well, and often substantially better than school kids on standardized tests, and hundreds of colleges—including highly selective institutions such as Stanford, Harvard, Yale, and the military service academies—welcome homeschoolers.

What about socialization?

The belief that socialization is a serious problem for homeschoolers is a complete delusion. Instead of spending the major portion of their day in a closed room with twenty-five children of roughly the same age and knowledge level and one adult to oversee them, homeschooled kids have the time and freedom to interact with people of all ages and types, to learn to deal with them as individuals.

Some critics of homeschooling contend that by not attending school, homeschooled kids lack the opportunity to learn to deal with bullies and hazing. Most homeschooling parents would counter that the world offers enough opportunities to learn to cope with unpleasant people that we don't need to deliberately subject them to such situations. Outside the peer-driven classroom, homeschooled kids develop confidence in their own personalities and abilities. Many homeschoolers tend not just to tolerate differences among individuals but to actively cultivate and enjoy them.

Finding the right curriculum was challenging, but once we found it, the experience has been satisfying.

Nash, father of Jimmy, 3, and Colt, 10

Homework

Our daughter was craving homework. She'd watched her older sisters do it for years and used to pretend to do it. We bought her pencils, drawing paper, crayons, lined paper, glue, and everything else she wanted. By the time she got to preschool, homework was anticlimactic.

Won, mother of
Camille, 7,
Tess, 10, and
Emily, 15

Years ago, knowing that Bernie and I would soon be parents of a kindergartner, our friends with older children felt oddly compelled to share some of the unpleasantness their children had encountered. One day when Bernie, Alex, and I went on a walk in the mountains with some friends who had children, my conversation with Ian, a public broadcasting producer I'd known for years, typified the problem.

As we walked together trailing the larger group, Ian turned to me and said, "Be prepared for homework."

"Homework?" I responded, with laughter. "You've got to be kidding."

"Absolutely not," he said with his British accent intact after twenty years in the United States.

"What kind of homework can children do when they neither read nor write?"

"The dreaded bear project."

"What are you talking about?" I asked.

"It is quite possible that each Friday afternoon in every kindergarten classroom in the United States, one child is responsible for bringing home a teddy bear equipped with a backpack filled with clothes and a journal. It is the child's responsibility to include Teddy in all the family's weekend activities," he explained.

"Why would children have to do that?"

"The assumption is that it teaches them responsibility. I guess it depends on the child. A friend of ours told Hillary [his wife] that when her son Peter came home with Teddy, Peter threw Teddy in the closet and retrieved him on Monday morning. When his teacher asked, 'What did you and Teddy do this weekend?' Peter said he forgot, which would be possible if you knew Peter."

I laughed, knowing that this was irresponsible behavior, albeit funny. "What about Isabelle [his daughter]?"

"For someone who has never liked stuffed animals or dolls, her attentiveness to Teddy amazed and alarmed us. She brought this well-worn little chubby thing to every event we attended. Unfortunately, it was quite a busy weekend."

I smiled. He continued. "Friday night, Teddy went out to dinner with us. On Saturday he attended the screening of a children's film, during which Isabelle quietly explained the plot to him. On Sunday he joined us for brunch with Hillary's parents, who had just flown in from London. After the meal, they took Hillary aside and suggested we all return to England so that Isabelle could have a more normal and challenging educational experience. Sunday night, we attended my brother James's birthday party. Isabelle spent the entire evening talking with Teddy. She put him to bed, woke him up, and pretended to feed him from a bottle. James's single friends were astounded by Teddy's presence, continually lifting their eyebrows in puzzlement. They said nothing because they didn't want to hurt Isabelle's feelings, but they did sneak a lot of glances at us during the evening."

"I guess Teddy was one happy camper," I volunteered.

"He certainly was."

"What did Isabelle write in her journal?"

"As you succinctly stated earlier, she does not know how to write. However, she did paint a few colored abstract pictures, not intentionally, in which Teddy looked like a brown glob."

In the orientations when the teachers talked about homework, I laughed aloud, thinking it was a joke. My wife elbowed me in the ribs. I realized that no one else was laughing.

Jay, father of
Evie, 6

I laughed aloud.

Ian pretended to frown in response. "It's easy for you to laugh now, but just you wait."

As I was thinking about what he'd said, I tripped on a rock and skinned my knee. I immediately looked upward and said, "Okay, so I shouldn't have mocked Isabelle's assignment. I'm sorry. It was insensitive of me."

This time it was Ian's turn to laugh.

Bear Facts

Sherry Kaufman has taught kindergarten for twenty-five years, and Sandra Chon Wang has taught kindergarten for ten. They are both teachers at Westwood Charter Elementary School in Los Angeles, California.

While we're not sure you'll find a teddy bear in every classroom throughout the United States, it might be a good idea. Children universally love this assignment because it's fun. Teachers like it because it teaches the children literacy and responsibility.

The journal, which accompanies the bear, is an important literacy tool, a tangible example of the relationship between the spoken and the written word. As the weekend progresses, the children dictate their stories to their parents and watch their parents print their words in the children's journals. When the class hears them read the story aloud on Monday, it becomes a concrete and exciting way of seeing the connection between speaking, writing, reading, and listening.

The teddy bear project is also an invaluable way of teaching responsibility. In our classes, a child takes Teddy home after school on Friday and returns Teddy on Monday. Parents tell us that not only are their kindergartners serious about fulfilling their obligation to care for Teddy, but the project has additional values as well. In some families it's a way for siblings to share responsibility. In others, it's a family project, complete with photographs and all.

Susan, the mother of Drew, a special needs kindergartner, told us one of the most touching stories. It was the first month of school, which meant that only a few children had taken Teddy home. So when Drew's name was picked from the jar, which meant Teddy would be his weekend guest, Drew suddenly became a very important person.

Until that point, Susan said, Drew hadn't had a play date with any of the other kids, possibly because he wasn't very verbal and was quite shy. But Friday afternoon, after he became Teddy's guardian, Marc, another child in the class, approached Drew for a play date. As Susan honestly admitted, "Both Marc's mom and I knew that Marc had asked Drew for the play date solely so he could play with Teddy. What was amazing was that within thirty minutes of being home, the boys put Teddy on a chair in the corner and played with each other for the next two hours. Marc and Drew became fast friends . . . and it was all because of Teddy."

Greg, Julie's father, told us one of the most unusual stories about Teddy's adventure with their family. As the weekend progressed, Greg and his wife were proud of Julie's dedication to Teddy. Everything was working out fine until Julie took Teddy to her sister Lesley's high school basketball game. In the excitement of the moment, Julie must have knocked Teddy under the grandstands and forgotten about him. At bedtime, when Julie realized Teddy was gone, she sobbed herself to sleep.

Greg promised Julie that he would find Teddy the next morning. Lesley got a key to the gym from her coach. They drove to school to find Teddy, but he wasn't there. The coach called the school custodian at home, but he hadn't seen Teddy either. By this time, Greg told us he was so upset they'd lost Teddy that he went to six toy stores to see if he could find a Teddy look-alike, but there weren't any.

On Monday morning when Julie and Greg anxiously went to school to tell the teacher the sorrowful news, the teacher comforted them and took out another Teddy from the closet. It turned out this wasn't the first time Teddy had disappeared. Greg said he was so relieved he couldn't contain himself. Julie handled the whole trauma in a more adult manner.

Learning Responsibility

Denyse Anderson Lucas teaches kindergarten at the Morehead Elementary School in Greensboro, North Carolina.

My mother will attest to the fact that I certainly did not have homework in kindergarten. When Mom was in school, there *was* no such thing. In the years since kindergarten's inception, theories and practices have come full circle. If you have not been involved in a public school lately, or even if you have, you may have many questions about homework. Will my child come home with homework? Why? How much? What will it be like? Do I need to help?

Today's kindergartner will most likely come home with homework assignments. The emphasis is twofold. First is the responsibility of bringing the work home, bringing it back to school on time, and making sure it finds its way to the correct place in the classroom. Forming this habit early is invaluable to parents and students in later years. Chances are, your child's teacher is going to forgive tactical mistakes in the beginning as this is an important learning time for both you and your child. This skill will develop with help from you and the teacher. Second, homework serves as a link between home and school. Through your child's assignments you should be able to see what is being covered in class. Homework is generally given as a reinforcement for skills introduced and practiced at school. You may also be able to tell if your child is mastering the skill that is being reinforced. This is an important time for you both. Taking homework seriously shows your child that you take school seriously and that you believe it is important.

Our son's homework takes about ten minutes a night. It's no big deal.

Laurie, mother of
Byron, 5

Assignments will be very basic, although a good teacher will find ways to make them creative. In the beginning, it is likely that your child will practice writing and naming letters, writing and naming numbers, and performing simple math functions. As the year progresses your child will move on to writing words and then sentences and reading small books appropriate to his or her ability. Often, teachers will ask students to collect objects or make observations related to the current unit of study, for example, collecting leaves or insects, or perhaps keeping a calendar of the week's weather.

Your child will need your help for doing kindergarten homework. Set a certain time each afternoon or evening for working together. You will probably need to read directions and guide your child through the activity. However, allow your child to do his or her own work and to make mistakes. Your child will undoubtedly learn from them. If your child regularly struggles with homework, set a stopping time. Twenty minutes is usually enough time to complete an assignment. If your child becomes frustrated, take a break and try again later. Five math problems done correctly are worth more than a page of problems and a frustrated child in tears.

If homework becomes a struggle, or on the other hand, is not challenging your child, talk to the teacher for additional ideas on how to make homework time more valuable. It is his or her job to modify homework when necessary to make it more or less challenging.

Most important, consider it *your* homework to make a good impression on your child. Make certain that your child observes you reading, writing, and using math at home. Whether it is making a grocery list, reading a magazine, or figuring out the tip at a dinner out, you are the most influential teacher in your child's life.

It seems to be "much ado about nothing."

Lupi, mother of Paloma, 5, and Jovany, 8

Kindergarten Readiness

‑ ‑

W hen Alex was in preschool, one of the boys was held back from kindergarten because of impulse control problems; he hit other kids—a lot. Later I learned that while this behavior was over the top, it was one of many signs of a lack of kindergarten readiness. More common indicators include an inability to concentrate on tasks, listen to stories, or follow directions. Some children don't do well in group activities or find it difficult to transition from one task to another.

However, the most common reason for delaying kindergarten entrance is chronological age. If a child's birth date is close to the cutoff date, which varies from state to state, some parents feel that the age variance will cause their child to lag behind. Others think that an extra year in preschool will give their child an edge in kindergarten, although research doesn't bear this out.

For Gail and Kevin, parents of Aaron, a late-birthday kid, the issues were clear but the resolution wasn't. "Not only would Aaron have been one of the youngest children in his

W ho's ever ready for kindergarten? My mother says that I was a real baby.

Bart, father of
Meredith, 7

class," Gail said, "but he is physically small, only in the fortieth percentile."

"But he's smart as a whip," Kevin interjected. "His preschool had begun boring him to tears. He hated playing in the sandbox and making the same arts and crafts projects over and over. He is intellectually curious. He knew his letters and numbers. His older sisters had taught him how to spell. He was clearly ready for a more academic program."

"But we had concerns," Gail said. "I was afraid he'd be lost in the crowd. You only know how smart he is if you take the time to talk with him. Otherwise he seems withdrawn."

"And because of his size, I worried he'd be bullied," Kevin said. "I had skipped a grade when I was in grade school and it was a big mistake. I was smart enough to be with older kids, but less physically and socially mature. I regretted it until college."

"So we were unsure what to do," Gail continued. "The preschool director said Aaron was ready for kindergarten, but we weren't convinced."

"We also knew that no matter what we decided, we wouldn't want him to stay in the same preschool. He'd not only progressed way beyond it, but we felt there would be a stigma if he were held back," Kevin said.

"I'd visited a number of kindergarten classes," Gail interjected, "and the more I saw, the less convinced I was that Aaron would fit in. I was at my wit's end when a friend recommended a prekindergarten program. Her daughter was vivacious and outgoing, also very smart, but somewhat immature."

"Initially I was against even pursuing this option," Kevin responded. "I worried that a transition program like this would be geared to misfits or kids who were slow, but we were totally surprised."

"The program was exceptional," Gail agreed. "Most of the kids were bright, just young. Some had maturity problems; others, including Aaron, didn't do very well in physical activities. A few had learning disabilities but were still quite intelligent.

> *Warren cried for the first few days. His teacher said he was withdrawn for the next week. I was just about ready to see the principal when he hit another kid. Now I knew he was feeling at home.*
>
> Rochelle, mother of Warren, 7

"The director was dynamic and the teachers were first-rate. The program's goal was to provide a stimulating learning environment that was developmentally appropriate for each child, not to replicate the kindergarten curriculum."

"It was the best decision we could have made," Kevin said. "Aaron flourished. He developed more self-confidence and has become more outgoing. He's now in the forty-sixth percentile of height."

"Two of his new friends will be in his kindergarten class next year," Gail enthusiastically said. "The whole ordeal turned out for the best. He finally seems happy."

Kevin and Gail looked at each other and sighed with relief.

Ready or Not

Robert S. Byrd, M.D., M.P.H., is an assistant professor in the Department of Pediatrics at the UC Davis School of Medicine.

What do you think of kindergarten readiness testing?

If parents have made the right choices in raising their children, they won't be in a quandary about when to send them to kindergarten. Generally, a child is not ready for school if he has been in an environment for five years that hasn't helped him get ready for school. When a school administrator or a kindergarten teacher says to the parents of that child, "He is not ready for school. Go home and have him come back in a year," they are not addressing the child's needs.

School may very well be the right place for a child whose emotional, behavioral, and cognitive developmental level is deemed not ready. Enrolling that child in school, or actively working with him to develop the appropriate skills and abilities for school, may be the best option. Giving him a readiness test that he will undoubtedly fail will not help his self-esteem.

Instead of being told, "Come to school; it's a wonderful place," what you're saying to that child is, "You're not good enough for school. When you're a year older, perhaps you will then be able to compete with children who are not your age."

What is the rationale for delaying kindergarten for one year?

It ranges. Some parents think their child will have an extra advantage if he or she is more mature, taller, older. When one looks closely at the school cutoff dates, the age-range difference within a kindergarten class should be at most a year. When children are held back, the disparities are even greater.

The expectation of all parents is that they want their children to be challenged. However, asking the teacher to challenge both the six-year-olds and five-year-olds is a difficult task. What is challenging for a five-year-old will probably be easy for a six-year-old. What is appropriate for a six-year-old may be overwhelming for a five-year-old.

In my current research project, we are focusing on dropout rates among eighth-graders who begin school later, fail a grade, or are age-appropriate for their grade level. The children who are older than their peers risk having behavior problems in adolescence. Being older seems to set up a dynamic that may not be healthy, although the full reasons for this are not understood. Still, this preliminary information allows us to question the value of holding children back, which has become a widespread practice, although there is no data to support its effectiveness.

When should parents hold their child back?

Holding a child back is appropriate if you, your child's preschool director, or the administrators at your new elementary school think your child is not ready. In that case, the most positive way to handle the situation is to ask the elementary school administrator, what shall we do to get my child ready for school? How shall we address the issues in an active way (rather than passively sitting and hoping the problems will

Kamal was so ready, it made me feel bad.

Andrea, mother of Kamal, 6

resolve themselves over the course of a year). In some cases, the passing of time may be the best solution, but that decision should be made only after careful consideration of the child's strengths and needs and the options available.

What can we, as parents, do to help prepare our children for kindergarten?

First, read to your kids every day. Read in a way that is enjoyable for both you and them. Second, play with your child, because children learn through play. What's important here is to figure out ways to play so that your child can learn without feeling it's a test. If you and your child have been playing with magnetic letters or you have been taking a walk in the neighborhood looking for letters on street signs and buildings and you finish the activity and say, "Okay, now I'm going to quiz you on your alphabet," then you are defeating your own purpose.

Third, limit television. TV is a passive activity that is high in stimulation. There is constant action, which children find appealing, but it decreases their attention span. When your child starts school, you don't want him or her to have unrealistic expectations. During the day your child's teacher will not be replaced by a cast of other teachers. There will be no scene changes, and the teacher will not have background music to focus the children's attention. The hours a day that kids sit in front of television means that they are not involved in other activities, like cutting and pasting, reading, learning to play with other kids, learning how to fight and make up, building with blocks, exploring their world, and practicing their language.

Fourth, send your child to preschool. It helps you evaluate how he or she will do in a classroom setting and allows you a year to identify and address any special needs that a child may have. Finally, remember that kindergarten can be a wonderful experience for your child, particularly if you are an active participant, someone your child can count on for support, encouragement, and acceptance.

Neither of our girls had any separation problems. They spent two years in full-day preschool.

Garry, father of
Heidi, 5, and
Jaclyn, 12

The Importance of Preschool

Edward F. Zigler, Ph.D., is the Sterling Professor of Psychology at Yale University, the director of the Bush Center on Child Development and Social Policy, and is a founder of Head Start.

Why should children attend preschool?

The primary reason for attending preschool is to learn the types of social skills and cognitive literacy that are necessary when a child gets to elementary school. The purpose of preschool is primarily for school readiness, but it is also the foundation that prepares a child for life after school as well. What kind of person you are and what values you have are determined in those critical first few years of life. For example, among the areas in which young children have to develop is what we call emotional regulation so they don't act out and have temper tantrums. We expect this of a two-year-old but not of a four-year-old. The skills children learn in preschool, such as impulse control, are important later in life, not just in school. Those first few years are important years for the development of character and personality.

How should preschool differ from kindergarten?

Learning in preschool and kindergarten falls on a continuum. Children are taught skills in motor development, cognitive development, and motivational development. The teaching of these skills begins in preschool and continues into kindergarten. There is no great dramatic change in a child's life when he or she moves from being four years eleven months to being five years old. Between beginning preschool and beginning kindergarten, children develop and mediate their world with a different cognitive system than they had earlier. We call this developing maturity. Children are somewhat more mature in kindergarten. They can handle more frustration; they have better attention spans so teachers can do more involved projects with them in kindergarten than in preschool.

How much preschool does a child need?

In terms of learning social skills, two years of preschool would be ideal. In fact, in France and Italy, school starts at three. In this country, we argue about whether kids need two years or one year of preschool. In terms of cognitive development, the evidence shows that two years certainly appears better than one, particularly for children who are growing up in poverty.

For the first few weeks I was worried about our son, Andy, because he cried each morning when I dropped him off and each afternoon when I picked him up. His teacher assured me that he stopped crying the moment he walked in the classroom and started again when he was lining up to come home. You can't imagine my relief when he stopped altogether.

Leslie, mother of
Andy, 5

What criteria should parents look for in choosing a preschool?

One of the most important criteria is the child-staff ratio. Make sure there are not more than ten children per teacher; seven would be better. The next criterion is the training of the preschool teacher. Preferably we would like somebody with a B.A. in early childhood education. If not that, then a child development associate degree or an A.A. degree. The training of the teacher is important. How much experience has the teacher had?

What is the philosophy of the preschool? Do they have a curriculum that is in line with your education philosophy? There are schools with curricula that stretch from what we call structured (rigorous fill-in-the-lines and workbooks) to unstructured (play-oriented). Parents need to decide which kind of preschool they think is best for their child, although they have to be careful. If anything, parents tend to want too much structure. That is why my colleague David Elkind wrote his books *The Hurried Child: Growing Up Too Fast Too Soon* and *Miseducation: Preschoolers at Risk*.

There is so much emphasis on cognitive development and school readiness that parents forget that this is the time when children are developing their character and social skills, which are just as important in life as their IQs. I warn parents to make sure they are not sending their child to a preschool that is teaching a first-grade curriculum to three-year-olds.

Children develop at their own pace, and you can overburden them just like you can overburden adults. They can become too stressed out. I tend to agree with David Elkind that we are probably pushing children too fast, too hard, and too early. It can turn them off to school. Too much structure also denies them their childhood. Childhood isn't supposed to be busy-work every minute of the day. When do children have time to lie on their backs, chew on a blade of grass, and look at the clouds passing overhead? That's part of growing up and learning too.

Learning

My daughter was a top-notch student from day one. Our son had problems from kindergarten through first grade. His second-grade teacher figured it out. She said that he learns by doing, not by reading. She changed the way she taught him and suddenly he felt successful for the first time.

Jim, father of
Daniel, 7, and
Cassie, 10

"I never thought too much about how children learn," said Anna, the mother of three. "When our oldest daughter, Emily, was in kindergarten, my husband, Franco, and I thought only about teaching rather than learning. We figured if the teacher was good, Emily would learn.

"It wasn't until second grade that we were introduced to the concept of learning styles. Emily's teacher, who was wonderful, explained that children learn in different ways and in different environments. Some are visual, some are tactile, and some are kinesthetic—they learn by doing. Certain children like quiet environments and others learn better with groups of kids. The point is that if you recognize children's learning styles, you can teach to their strengths. Of course, it's also important to broaden their exposure so that they can adapt to other teachers and other classroom experiences.

"Once she said that, I realized that when I volunteered in the classroom I had seen differences among children. I didn't grasp what they meant. Now that Emily is in the fourth grade, and sometimes does homework with her friends at our house, the differences are obvious. For example, I know that Emily learns visually. Give her books and written assignments, and she's off on her own. Her best friend, Kimi, seems to learn through osmosis, although heaven only knows how. She's got a great sense of imagination, and just when you're sure she's accomplished nothing because she was daydreaming, she sits down and completes the entire assignment without a moment's hesitation.

"When our twins, Dante and Giancarlo, were born, from the beginning Franco and I immediately recognized their differences. Dante was quiet and easy to take care of. When Giancarlo cried, which was often, you could hear his screams two states away.

"By the time the boys were in preschool, we could tell that Giancarlo was a kinesthetic learner; he's very physical and needs to be active. Dante learns by listening. And although preschool teachers are not supposed to have favorites, most of the teachers liked Dante better because he does the work he's supposed to, he's neat, and he follows directions well.

"Giancarlo is a far greater challenge. He's easily bored and he shows no hesitancy in expressing his feelings aloud. When he likes to do something, he does it well. When he's disinterested, he doesn't. He's far more difficult to "control" than Dante. However, once you realize his strengths, you can easily win him over if you present challenges in a different way. The one preschool teacher who understood Giancarlo was totally taken with him.

"Since the boys have just started kindergarten, it's difficult to evaluate how they're doing. Franco and I just hope that each of the boys' teachers will appreciate him for who he is."

When you have an only child, it's difficult to know how to compare him. Our son started out a little slowly, and I think I had a weekly conference with his teacher. About midway through, he suddenly found himself and did well.

Sandra, mother of Sandy, 8

What Should Young Children Be Learning?

Lilian G. Katz is the director of the ERIC Clearinghouse on Elementary and Early Childhood Education and professor emerita at the University of Illinois at Urbana-Champaign.

Research on intellectual and social development and learning is rich in implications for curriculum and teaching strategies for early childhood education. Unfortunately, educational practices tend to lag behind what is known about teaching and learning.

THE NATURE OF DEVELOPMENT

The concept of development includes two dimensions: the normative dimension, concerning the capabilities and limitations of most children at a given age, and the dynamic dimension, concerning the sequence and changes that occur in all aspects of the child's functioning as he or she grows. While the normative dimension indicates what children can and cannot do at a given age, the dynamic dimension raises questions about what children should or should not do at a particular time in their development in light of possible long-term consequences.

In many kindergartens, young children are engaged in filling out worksheets, reading from flash cards, or reciting numbers by rote. But just because young children can do those things in a normative sense is not sufficient justification for requiring them to do so. Young children usually willingly do most things adults ask of them. But their willingness is not a reliable indicator of the value of an activity. The developmental question is not "What can children do?" Rather, it is "What should children do that best serves their learning and development in the long term?"

LEARNING THROUGH INTERACTION

Contemporary research confirms the view that young children learn most efficiently when they are engaged in interaction rather than in merely receptive or passive activities. Young children should be interactive with adults, materials, and their surroundings in ways that help them make sense of their own experience and environment. They should be investigating and observing aspects of their environment worth learning about and recording their findings and observations through talk, paintings, and drawings. Interaction that arises in the course of such activities provides a context for much social and cognitive learning.

FOUR CATEGORIES OF LEARNING

The four categories of learning outlined below are especially relevant to the education of young children.

Knowledge. In early childhood, knowledge consists of facts, concepts, ideas, vocabulary, and stories. A child acquires knowledge from someone's answers to his or her questions, explanations, descriptions, and accounts of events as well as through observation.

Skills. Skills are small units of action that occur in a relatively short period of time and are easily observed or inferred. Physical, social, verbal, counting, and drawing are among a few of the almost endless number of skills learned in the early years. Skills can be learned from direct instruction and improved with practice and drill.

Dispositions. Dispositions are thought of as habits of mind or tendencies to respond to certain situations in certain ways. Curiosity, friendliness or unfriendliness, bossiness, and creativity are dispositions or sets of dispositions rather than skills or pieces of knowledge. There is a significant difference between having writing skills and having the disposition to be a writer.

Dispositions are not learned through instruction or drill. The dispositions that children need to acquire or strengthen—curiosity, creativity, cooperation, and friendliness—are learned primarily from being around people who exhibit them. It is unfortunate that some dispositions, such as being curious or puzzled, are rarely displayed by adults in front of children.

A child who is to learn a particular disposition must have the opportunity to behave in a manner that is in keeping with the disposition. If that occurs, then the child's behavior can be responded to, and thus strengthened. Teachers can reinforce certain dispositions by setting learning goals rather than performance goals. A teacher who says, "Let's see how much we can find out about something," rather than, "I want to see how well you can do," encourages children to focus on what they are learning rather than on their performance.

Feelings. These are subjective emotional states, many of which are innate. Among those that are learned are feelings of competence, belonging, and security. Feelings about school, teachers, learning, and other children are also learned in the early years.

VARIETY OF TEACHING METHODS

It is reasonable to assume that when a single teaching method is used for a diverse group of children, a significant proportion of these children is likely to fail. For younger children, a greater variety of teaching methods should be utilized, since the younger the group is, the less likely the children are to have been socialized into a standard way of responding to their environment, and it is more likely that the children's readiness to learn is influenced by background experiences that are idiosyncratic and unique.

Our children's learning ability depended upon their teacher's teaching ability.

Linda, mother of
Stacy, 6, Nicole, 8,
and Taylor, 12

For practical reasons there are limits as to how varied teaching methods can be. It should be noted, however, that while approaches dominated by workbooks often claim to individualize instruction, they really individualize nothing more than the days on which a child completes a routine task. Such programs can deaden the disposition to learn.

As for the learning environment, the younger the children are, the more informal it should be. Informal learning environments encourage spontaneous play, in which children engage in whatever play activities interest them. Such activities may include group projects, investigations, constructions, and dramatic play.

Spontaneous play is not the only alternative to early academic instruction. The data on children's learning suggests that kindergarten experiences require an intellectually oriented approach in which children interact in small groups as they work together on projects that help them make sense of their own experience. These projects should also strengthen their dispositions to observe, experiment, inquire, and examine the worthwhile aspects of their environment more closely.

Teaching and Learning

Arlene Garbus has been a teacher at Westwood Charter Elementary School in Los Angeles, California, for more than thirty years.

When I began teaching, I was certain that if I skillfully presented a thoughtfully developed and interesting curriculum, my students would learn. Most of them did. Still, with increased experience, I began to understand that teaching is only one component of the equation; the other is learning.

Long before professors in teacher education training programs delineated the different ways in which children learn, those of us who taught day after day already had figured this out. Whether or not we were able to define and articulate these learning styles, we knew they were there because we learned from our students.

As I watched the children in my classroom develop skills, learn concepts, and—even on a basic level—begin to understand the connections and interrelationships between concepts, I could see that they processed information in different ways. No matter what I presented, children assimilated it in unique ways.

For example, if I was doing a science lesson on the weather, I knew that Darren would look at printed words (even if he didn't yet know how to read), drawings, or the computer monitor. Maya would walk outside, look at the sky, come inside, and dance.

All these years later, I remember a child named Rebecca, who was very quiet and somewhat of an enigma to me. One day when it was raining, she stood alone in a corner and qui-

What can I say? My daughter's kindergarten made learning such a wonderful adventure that when my daughter couldn't go to school because she was sick, she cried.

Lorraine, mother
of Maggie, 6

etly recited a poem titled "The Rain," from Jack Prelutsky's *Read-Aloud Rhymes for the Very Young.* I asked her if she would like to recite it again in front of the class. She thought a moment, and much to my surprise, said yes. I asked all the other children to stop what they were doing and listen to Rebecca. She remained in her corner but looked at the class, and in a quiet but firm voice said "Rain on the green grass, and rain on the tree, and rain on the housetop, but not upon me." The children clapped, and the smile on Rebecca's face brought tears to my eyes.

It is the challenge of discovering how a child learns best and allowing for his or her individuality that makes teaching such a rewarding profession.

Math

"When Robin was in preschool, we had no idea how good she was in math," said Gabrielle, the mother of a blended family. "My ex-husband and I thought she could count only to twenty because she'd never counted any higher for us. My second husband is a widower with children. Once I remarried and Robin had older siblings around, we learned she could count to one hundred. The only way we found out was because her seven-year-old stepbrother Brad and eleven-year-old stepsister Pennie told us. Robin is evidently a competitive mathematician. When Brad bragged how high he could count, Robin revealed her talent. When I asked Robin why she hadn't told me before, she said it was because I had never asked. Boy, did I feel guilty.

"When Robin entered kindergarten, it became clear she had better math skills than many of her classmates. My friend Kathy told me her daughter Marisa could barely count to ten, but she was very creative when she played with her dolls. Eddie's mother, Arlene, said Eddie could count, but he couldn't write, so what difference did it make?

"What is so curious to me is that Robin has no genetic predisposition for math. I consider myself mathematically illiterate. It's not that I'm not smart; I have a master's degree in

I used to be good at math until the seventh grade, when girls typically weren't supposed to be good any more. But things have changed and Samantha has a real facility for it, even when she was in kindergarten.

Erica, mother of Samantha, 10

English literature. It's just that I have math anxiety. I'm not convinced that my ex-husband, who graduated from college with a degree in communications, can even add. Of course, that's an ex-wife's opinion.

"Anyway, from the start Robin's kindergarten teacher realized that she was capable in math. Robin knew how to count by twos, sort by shapes, and classify objects. Since there were three other children who were at Robin's level, they worked together on more complex problems. The teacher called this individualization, which means a child is taught at his or her level of ability rather than grade level.

"My only concern was that if Robin moved above grade level in kindergarten, she would be bored in first grade. But her teacher assured me that this wasn't the case. In first grade, she was in a combined class of first- and second-grade children. In second grade it was the same, only here she was able to help the younger children who needed it. That was good because it taught her patience.

"The only remaining problem is that I think I'll reach my mathematical peak when Robin's in high school. It's just lucky my husband excels in this area and so do my stepchildren. Still, I'm considering taking a remedial math class at a local high school adult program because I'm beginning to feel humbled. Robin promises she'll help me with my homework, and I guess that's good. But whoever thought I'd be tutored in math by my nine-year-old? Yikes!"

Discovering Math

Douglas H. Clements, Ph.D., is a professor of learning and instruction at the State University of New York at Buffalo.

How much math should prekindergartners know?

Ideally, early childhood teachers should not expect children starting kindergarten to have mastered a set of skills, particularly since individual and cultural differences affect children's learning experiences. According to the National Council of Teachers of Mathematics, of which I am a member, a firm foundation in numbers and geometry are solid goals for the prekindergarten child.

In our Building Blocks project at the State University of New York at Buffalo, we have the same expectations. We specify goals for young children without trying to create rigid expectations for a given grade level. Nonetheless, one thing is certain: most children have mathematical competencies and abilities that surpass what is often believed by adults.

In Building Blocks, we work in numbers with pre-K age children to develop the ability to

- count objects (rational counting) to ten (or more) with understanding

- count aloud (rote counting) to thirty or more

- know the "next number" to ten

- subitize—instantly recognize—small groups of objects to three, four, or five

- use counting to compare sets (more/fewer)

- solve simple, concrete addition problems with small numbers

- share objects among several people

In geometry, we are working with pre-K kids to help them develop the ability to

- recognize shapes, even nonprototypical or nonstandard shapes

- put shapes together to make other shapes

- use very simple map ideas to navigate

- determine congruent shapes

- match lengths

It is important to note that many of these goals are introduced to pre-K students and continue well into the kindergarten year.

What constitutes a good mathematics program?

For early childhood, quality mathematics is about challenge and joy, not imposition and pressure. Good early childhood mathematics is broader and deeper than practicing counting and adding. It includes discussions about which child is bigger and drawing maps to the treasure buried outside. Quality mathematics instruction includes providing a large quantity of unit blocks, with adequate time to use them, asking children to get just enough pencils for everyone in their group, and challenging children to estimate and check how many steps it is to the playground.

Everything around us can be better understood with mathematics. Preschool and kindergarten are good times for children to become interested in counting, sorting, building shapes, patterning, measuring, and estimating. Quality kindergarten mathematics is not a watered-down version of high-level math. Instead, it invites children to experience mathematics as they play in, describe, and think about their world.

Kindergartners actively construct mathematical knowledge. So do people of all ages, but kindergartners are a special group, and we need to plan instruction with care. Consider two of their special characteristics. First, the ideas kindergartners construct are uniquely different from those of adults. Early childhood teachers must be particularly careful not to assume that children "see" situations, problems, or solutions as they do. Successful teachers interpret what the child is doing and thinking and attempt to see the situation from the child's point of view. Based on their interpretations, they conjecture what the child might be able to learn or abstract from his or her experiences. Similarly, when they interact with the child, they also consider their own actions from the child's point of view. This makes early childhood teaching both demanding and rewarding.

Second, young children do not act as if their world were divided into separate cubbyholes since they do not perceive it that way. Successful kindergarten teachers help children develop premathematical and mathematical knowledge

Our son Nick also could do double-digit addition before he entered kindergarten. His older sister taught him, but I think that he may be gifted in this area.

Victor, father of Nick, 5, Lisa, 8, and Ryan, 10

throughout the day. They plan activities that simultaneously help develop children intellectually, socially, emotionally, and physically. When kindergartners do mathematics, they do it by acting with their whole beings.

Such holistic teaching capitalizes on kindergartners' high level of motivation to learn and practice competencies in a self-directed manner. It provides a picture of mathematics as a positive, self-motivated, self-directed, problem-solving activity at the time children first develop their mathematical beliefs, habits, and feelings.

It follows that children's play and interests are the sources of their first mathematical experiences. These experiences become mathematical as they are represented and reflected upon. Young children represent their ideas by talking, but also through models, dramatizations, and art. From the motoric and singsong beginnings of "pat-a-cake" stem the geometric patterns of a "fence" built from unit blocks and the gradual generalization and abstraction of patterns throughout the child's day: "See, my drawing uses an ABAAB pattern like your blocks did this morning!"

Quality learning is often incidental and informal. This does not mean it is unplanned or unsystematic. It does mean that the role of the teachers is complex.

Math and Science

Sarah Kalsem, an elementary teacher at Shimek Elementary School in Iowa City, Iowa, and Thomas Rocklin, a professor of educational psychology at the University of Iowa, have collaborated on the Developmental Activities Program (DAP) at Shimek.

The cornerstone of our math and science program is a curriculum called DAP, which was developed by Darrell Phillips of the University of Iowa (darrell-phillips@uiowa.edu) and Dale Phillips of the Grantwood Area Education Agency.

DAP is strongly based on Piagetian ideas about cognitive development. Children actively construct knowledge in the form of logical structures, and the sequence in which these structures emerge is essentially fixed. For example, during the the fall semester of kindergarten, many of our children are developing early structures related to classification and ordering, as well as some basic number concepts.

During DAP time, children first choose a set of objects. Each set contains a large number of objects (buttons, toy animals, unit blocks, and many others). Children find a quiet place in the room where they can work without being bothered by others or bothering others. What they do with the materials is up to them. As they work, we circulate and work with one child at a time. We ask carefully chosen questions designed both to let us know what the child is thinking and to stimulate the child. For example, we might see that a child has sorted geometric shapes by color. After having the child describe what he or she has done, we might ask "Is there another way to sort them?"

The trick, of course, is asking the right questions. Choosing the right question depends on knowing where the child is developmentally, and knowing what the typical sequence of development is. Consider two children who have sorted some animals into a group of pigs and a group of horses. For one child, the appropriate question might be something like "Are there more pigs or more horses or just the same number?" For another, the appropriate question might be "Are there more pigs, or more animals?" The nature of DAP integrates instruction and assessment nearly completely. As we ask questions, we stimulate thought and learn about what the child can do. We keep notes on each interaction, so we can see the progress each child is making.

Multicultural
Education

"Anika's experience in kindergarten was a breeze," her mother, Janice, said. (Janice is Caucasian and her husband, Mark, is African American.) "Our elementary school is in our neighborhood. We already knew some of the other children and their parents from preschool. Her teacher was warm and nurturing. While the school is predominantely Caucasian, Anika, like Mark and me, has always been comfortable in both the Caucasian and African American worlds.

"The elementary school curriculum, like that at most schools, is not an integrated multicultural one. Still, during the year there are some multicultural activities. At our school we celebrate everyone's background—whether their parents or grandparents are from Europe, the Middle East, Africa, Japan, China, or Australia. So Anika has always felt comfortable. What's interesting to Mark and me is that some years she celebrates her African American heritage and others she celebrates the Russian heritage of my grandparents.

"In terms of her friends, she's always been happy and popular. Surprisingly enough, most of her problems and ours have been with teachers. What always surprises us is when Anika, now eleven, is expected to be the classroom

One generation makes all the difference. My wife and I are college-educated professionals who were born in the United States. My parents came from Japan and hardly spoke English. When I was young, I was embarrassed because my parents followed the old customs and we ate food that was different from our friends. Now everyone eats sushi.

Michael, father of
Jonathan, 5, and
Andrew, 7

We are African American and our children go to a school that is split fairly evenly between African Americans, Koreans, and Latinos. Kindergarten is an unusual time because the children literally see no difference. Too bad the parents do.

Chris, father of Randy, 15 months, David, 5, and Laura, 8

authority on African American history, culture, and music. If the class is given an essay to write on slavery, usually she is the only child picked to read hers aloud. In one case, when she had a particularly disagreeable teacher who clearly had major problems, racism being only one, I wanted to pull Anika out of the class and transfer her to another one. But she wanted to stay because her best friends were in the class. My husband and I were very unhappy, but we let her make the decision.

"It's obvious that Anika's situation is much different from that of other children we know in other places in the country. We live in a large urban city that is very diverse. We have friends of all ethnicities and religions."

Some family friends, the Grants, where the mother is a professor and the father is a doctor, moved from New York to a midsize city in another part of the country because of their job opportunities. After four years, their kids are not at all happy. Some of the children with whom they go to school had never known an African American child before they met the Grant kids. In kindergarten, because of their physical differences, the Caucasian kids wanted to touch the Grant children's hair and compare skin colors. While it was fine in kindergarten, as the kids got older and there were children in their class that they didn't know, they began feeling the racial element of the experience. The children are begging to return to New York, and their parents are seriously considering it.

"In Anika's case, the only troubling situation for her occurred in kindergarten. One day, Anika came home from school and was clearly upset. When I asked why, she said, 'Kimberly [a little girl in her class] said my skin is chocolate.'

"She had tears in her eyes and said, 'Mommy, I don't look chocolate, do I?'

"'No, sweetie,' I replied. 'You just look like your father's and my beautiful daughter.'

"She hugged me and went outside to play."

Equity and Excellence

James A. Banks is professor and director of the Center for Multi-cultural Education at the University of Washington, Seattle. His books include *An Introduction to Multicultural Education: Teaching Strategies for Ethnic Studies; Cultural Diversity and Education: Teaching Strategies for Social Studies;* and *Educating Citizens in a Multicultural Society.*

What are the major issues in a multicultural approach to learning for kindergartners?

The two major issues that teachers should be aware of in a multicultural approach to kindergarten education are research on the racial attitudes of children and research on ways to help children develop more positive racial and ethnic attitudes.

Many teachers with whom I have talked in university classes and school district workshops have stated that young children are unaware of racial and ethnic differences. These teachers believe that young children don't "see" the colors of various racial and ethnic groups and are, therefore, reluctant to teach young children about racial and ethnic differences because they may destroy their racial and ethnic innocence. Teachers who express these feelings believe that teachers should try to make children color-blind on issues related to race and ethnicity.

There are a number of problems with a "color-blind" approach to race and ethnic issues in early childhood educa-tion. One major problem with this approach is that it is incon-sistent with reality. Research has established, during a period that extends over fifty years, that young children are aware of racial and ethnic differences and have internalized the domi-nant society's norms about the social status of different racial and ethnic groups. The racial attitudes of young children mir-ror those of adults in U.S. society. By the age of four, young children are aware of racial differences and have attitudes that reflect those of adults in society. In racial attitude studies with young children from all racial and ethnic groups, they tend to express a white preference and to prefer white to brown.

There are other problems with the color-blind approach to race relations. Research shows that teachers who said they were color-blind actually discriminated against African American students in the school. They said they didn't see color, yet suspended African American boys at a highly disproportionate rate. They also did not incorporate content about African Americans into the school curriculum. Consequently, one of the problems with a color-blind stance is that teachers may not be aware of the way in which they are discriminating against students of color. The color-blind stance is a way to avoid dealing with racial problems and issues in the curriculum and in the school.

How should kindergarten teachers change the curriculum so that children from different cultures can succeed?

Research indicates that teachers can help students develop more positive and democratic racial attitudes by using multicultural teaching materials and approaches. These studies provide guidelines that can help kindergarten teachers improve intergroup relations in their classrooms and schools. In one of the earliest curriculum studies, conducted in 1952, researchers found that a democratic, multicultural curriculum had a positive effect on the racial attitudes of both the students and teachers. A later study found that white, second-grade children developed more positive racial attitudes after using multiethnic readers.

A longitudinal evaluation of *Sesame Street*, the multicultural television program for preschool children, supports the notion that multicultural materials and interventions can have a positive effect on the racial attitudes of young children. The investigators found that children who had watched the program for long periods had more positive racial attitudes toward outgroups than did children who had watched it for shorter periods.

Research indicates that curriculum interventions such as multicultural plays, folk dances, music, and role playing can also have positive effects on the racial attitudes of students. A curriculum intervention that consisted of folk dances, music, crafts, and role playing positively influenced the racial attitudes of students.

Kindergarten teachers can use the following guidelines to improve intergroup relations in their classrooms. These guidelines are discussed in more detail and with more examples in my book, *An Introduction to Multicultural Education*.

1. Select books and other teaching materials that include positive and realistic images of ethnic and racial groups in a consistent, natural, and integrated fashion. An excellent source of children's books to use in your classroom is *The New Press Guide to Multicultural Resources for Young Readers* by Daphne Muse. *Teaching Strategies for Ethnic Studies* by James A. Banks describes the histories and cultures of ethnic groups and includes annotations on books for children.

2. Involve students in vicarious experiences with different racial and ethnic groups. For example, use video clips and tapes, children's books, recordings, photographs, and other kinds of vicarious experiences to expose students to members of different racial and ethnic groups.

3. If you teach in an interracial school, involve students in structured interracial contact situations.

4. Involve students from different racial and ethnic groups in cooperative learning activities and in role playing and simulation activities.

When we first came from Vietnam, we kept our real names. The kids were laughed at and the parents couldn't seem to pronounce our names properly. Once we Americanized our names, there was no longer a problem.

Peter, father of
Ben, 6, Amanda, 8,
and Molly, 10

Music

In my son's class, they use songs for fun as well as learning. The teacher teaches them the days of the week through music. They also study Mozart and Beethoven.

Emil, father of
Daniel, 6

"I somehow remember your telling me that Mick's kindergarten teacher did something special with music?" I asked my friend Jordy, who's wanted to be a rock star since we were in college, and frequently talks like one, although he makes his living as a dentist.

"It was awesome!" he answered.

"In what way?"

"Have you ever thought, I mean seriously thought, about nose flutes?"

"Can't say that I have," I answered, with a chuckle.

"Then you're missing an entire musical tradition."

"Undoubtedly Jordy, but what's this got to do with kindergarten music?"

"Mick's teacher, Harley, was one bad dude. He had a cool collection of musical instruments. Nose flutes, bells, castanets, cymbals, a xylophone, kazoos, washboards, harmonicas, recorders, drums."

"And?"

"His curriculum was centered around music. He let the kids play the instruments they wanted to. They learned to read simple notes. He compared it to reading letters and words. Using musical themes, they celebrated tons of holidays from different cultures. That's how they learned geography."

"Sounds great."

"Yeah. They learned native dances, tap dances, and Gregorian chants. They made simple musical instruments, visited orchestras and choirs. Harley brought in videos of Kabuki theater, Nureyev and Fonteyn, African drum circles, and the Metropolitan Opera. His CD collection was outta sight. When Mick came home, he'd tell Sara and me about Mahalia Jackson, Mozart, Pavarotti, Willie Nelson, Yo-Yo Ma, Fats Waller, Beverly Sills, Bruce Springsteen, Joan Baez, Mick Jagger [his son's namesake], Beethoven, and the Beatles. And Mick knew their music."

"I'm impressed."

"Ya see, Suze," Jordy said, "Harley used music to develop community. I mean, here you got these people . . . and well . . . you know. Harley broke down barriers by inviting parents, grandparents, sisters, brothers, cousins, and friends to come to school to jam with the kids."

I nodded in agreement that this was a great idea.

"Yeah," Jordy said, almost to himself. "Classical musicians, guitarists, keyboard players, singers, dancers, drummers, and chanters. Awesome."

I smiled.

"You know," he said in a reflective tone, "many of Mick's best buds [he's in third grade] are from kindergarten. I think it's because," he paused for a long time, ". . . uh . . . they learned to see the world as a . . . um . . . giant conflagration of music, culture, song, and dance. Yeah."

After a moment I said, "What happened to Harley?"

"He moved to Louisiana and joined a Cajun band," Jordy said.

I burst out laughing.

If I hear one more nursery rhyme song, I'll scream. Isn't there more to music than "Old MacDonald," "The Farmer in the Dell," and "This Old Man"?

Delta, mother of Ross, 4, and Sharon, 6

The Sounds of Music

Larry Scripp, Ed.D., is chair of music education at the New England Conservatory and director of the Research Center for Learning through Music in Boston, Massachusetts. He also founded The Conservatory Lab Charter School for Learning Through Music.

What is the importance of music in kindergarten?

For kindergartners, music is an all-encompassing interest. They love music and many of their musical experiences are associated with home activities, such as watching TV, videotapes, or singing with their parents. The joy of music creates a comfortable bridge from what they learn at home to what they will be learning at school—particularly the concept of literacy. Knowing the words to a song is an introduction to literature. Understanding and liking music provides the background that will enhance the symbolic development of math and language.

Music is also important because it allows young children to anchor their focus on certain objects of study. A song that has lyrics that children enjoy singing over and over provides them with a consistent experience with certain structures of language. Knowing a song means knowing something about language. It means knowing something that can be shared because people can sing those songs together. They can change the words to the songs; they can sing it their own way as well as the way other people do. It provides limitless enjoyment.

What are the components of a good music program?

The goal of a good music program is to include music as an integral part of the curriculum.

- Students should be able to explore different kinds of instruments.
- They should have structured time to learn songs that will be part of their repertoire.

- Through music and dance programs, children can work on physical development and learn games that involve large and small motor skills.

- Exposing children to different kinds of music creates an aesthetic awareness.

- The music program should not be limited to nursery rhymes; it should include music from other parts of the world and different types of music, for example, classical music, indigenous ethnic (e.g., Balinese) music, contemporary music (Philip Glass, Bobby McFerrin, or Paul Winter), jazz improvisations of well-known songs such as "My Favorite Things," and high-quality children's music (Alex Willder Lullabies and Night Songs).

- A repetitive program—which does not include classics such as *The Nutcracker Suite*, which most kids love, and classical pieces they can readily understand and sing along with such as the Pachelbel Canon—provides limited exposure.

- Kindergarten is a good time for children to begin exploring representations of music. For example, you can teach music using the same principles as mathematics manipulatives. If kids are able to respond to symbols that have musical meanings, such as numbers, stick notations, and shapes, it helps them understand symbols that can be employed musically. It also ties into their literary development.

In our daughter's kindergarten, all the classes share a piano. While the teachers don't play very well, they're very enthusiastic. The kids think it's great.

> Manual, father of
> Jeremy, 7, and
> Lynne and
> Eddie, both 10

How are cutbacks affecting music education?

Dependent upon the budget, music programs come and go. In the last thirty or forty years, because of fluctuating funding, many people who enjoy music and understand its importance have created and sustained hundreds of community music schools.

There is a substantial population of kids who are getting music education one way or another by parents who insist on it. Parents who enjoy music themselves and want their children to develop an appreciation for it are sending their children to these schools or encouraging their kids to audition for children's choirs. Children whose parents don't like music, or who feel it takes away from serious subjects, are missing out.

If more parents understood that music can act as a catalyst for superior reading and writing, as well as emotional and physical development, they would not ignore this valuable resource.

The most important part of any music program is that there is a separate room for music.

Marianne, mother
of Cal, 1, and
Jack, 8

How can parents supplement a music program at home?

Do what we do at The Conservatory Lab Charter School, a school that is predicated on learning through music. Look at language development as a model. The optimum way of teaching children how to read is to expose them to books and to read to them. Music can be taught in the same way. Chances are that if your children have access to audiotapes or CDs, and if you listen to music with them and sing songs together, they'll learn that music is a joyful activity. If you teach your child to play simple instruments (or more complex ones that you know how to play), they will realize that music is a shared experience that family members can participate in together. If you're curious and willing to learn and explore different kinds of music, your children will follow your example.

Nonpublic Schools

"I must admit that I felt somewhat guilty when we decided to go the private school route," Stacy said. "Ernie [her husband] and I had always said we believe in public school. More than a year before it was time for Tori to start kindergarten, we visited our local school and didn't like it. We had already heard from neighborhood friends that the principal was 'weak,' and that, despite the efforts of some very committed teachers and parents, the curriculum was lackluster and teacher morale was low.

"While we could have looked at other public schools within our vicinity, for some reason we didn't. A number of children in our neighborhood were attending private schools. A few members of our weekly playgroup wanted to check them out. I went with them."

She sighed. "It was a big mistake, because after seeing the first school, I was hooked on the idea of private school, if not on the schools on our list. Out of the six schools my friends and I visited, there were two or three they seemed to like best. But I didn't feel any of them were right for Tori or for Ernie and me.

"Overall, my friends were looking for prestigious and exclusive schools with strong academic programs. Some wanted

Why did we send our children to private school? Because my husband and I both attended them ourselves and liked the environment.

Hogue, father of Lara, 8, and Miles, 10

I think Catholic schools are the best buy in town. The tuition is reasonable and the education is of high quality.

Rusty, father of
Scottie, 6, and
David, 9

to enroll their children in a school whose parents and children were 'right' for their family. A few were interested in schools whose graduates were almost assured admittance in a particular middle school, because the middle school admissions staff seemed to favor these children. Some were particularly interested in arts or sports programs.

"Ernie and I had some similar and some different objectives. Like the other parents, we knew that many of the private schools had smaller class sizes, stronger arts programs, more individualized attention, and more specialists in subjects like music, art, science, math, and physical education.

My greatest concern was educational philosophy. I was also interested in what the schools stood for, the academic background of the principal and teachers, class size, level of individualized help, and extracurricular activities.

"After I'd accumulated the data, Ernie and I visited my two favorite choices, which interestingly enough were at opposite ends of the spectrum. One was a progressive school, which means that the curriculum is somewhat determined by the students' interests. The learning is self-motivated. The teachers are considered facilitators. The emphasis is on nurturing the children's development rather than grading them. While ordinarily this would have been a little too unstructured for Ernie and me, it was sort of a modified version of what we had expected. The principal, teachers, and a curriculum consultant determined the academic program. A parents' committee participated in school governance.

"The role the children played was an integral part of the overall program, but not in the way we'd been led to believe.

"Actually, the entire concept made sense to me.

"The other school we were considering was a Roman Catholic school. While neither of us had attended church in many years, we are both Catholic and were aware of this school, although it's in another parish. What attracted me, and then us, to this particular school was all our usual criteria—small class size, strong teacher commitment, emphasis on basic skills, and academic excellence—but also the shared sense of values and beliefs.

"The principal was amazing. She had Ph.D.s in theology and education and spent alternate summers on religious retreats and building homes for Habitat for Humanity. We were truly impressed.

"Ultimately we decided upon the progressive school for Tori because we felt she needed a less structured environment. Two years later, we sent our son Jamie to the Catholic school because we knew it would be perfect for him. Both children are extraordinarily happy, and Ernie and I feel we made the right decisions."

Independent Schools

Peter Relic is the president of the National Association of Independent Schools.

What is the difference between independent and private schools?

Independent schools are part of the private or nonpublic school universe. The absence of tax dollars and church dollars differentiates the independent school from public and parochial schools. Independent schools rely primarily on tuition and gifts to the schools. Another difference is that independent schools are governed by a single board of trustees rather than having one board overseeing many schools, as in parochial diocesan schools. Thus, the primary differences between independent and religious schools revolve around governance and funding.

Why do parents send their children to independent or private schools?

Approximately three hundred thousand parents send their children to independent elementary schools, which are customarily defined as kindergarten through sixth grade. Gen-

Our kids go to a progressive school. It's more free-flowing, and children aren't so regimented. I must admit that I'm somewhat concerned about how they will adjust to the "real world."

Cosmo, father of Courtney, 5, and Creedence, 18

erally, parents are looking for a school that is consistent with their family values and attitudes and one that will best prepare their child for the future. More specifically, parents are looking for

- **Quality teaching.**
- **Small class size.** The National Association of Independent Schools (NAIS) suggests a student-teacher ratio of nine to one.
- **Safety.** Parents are increasingly concerned about violence and drug abuse.
- **Moral values, ethics, and social responsibility.**
- **A focused mission.** Parents want to know what population of students the school serves; for example, whether it is considered a college preparatory school or a school for special needs children (which many of the NAIS schools are). If they know what the school's mission is, they are better able to determine whether the school fits their requirements.
- **Individual counseling.** Parents want to be certain that a one-on-one relationship is being developed.
- **Equality in athletics and social activities.** Many independent schools encourage full student participation rather than allowing only the elite students onto the teams and into the clubs.

Two primary reasons: the arts and sports programs.

Sheila, mother of Julian, 7, Weaver, 9, and Rex, 15

How should parents evaluate nonpublic schools?

There is no easy answer to selecting the right private school for your child. Rankings, whether we're talking about elementary schools or college, often are based on superfluous criteria. Finding the right school is a much more complex process than reading rankings.

Everybody starts with reputation. People usually have some knowledge of schools based upon the school's reputation. Once parents have selected three or four schools that interest them, they should look at what the schools say about themselves—either in written material or on websites. How does the school evaluate itself? For what do they hold themselves accountable? In what ways will they allow parents to participate in the evaluation process? Are parents and their children allowed to visit the schools? May they spend a day talking to teachers, students, and administrators? If administrators say they are too busy and don't welcome prospective children and their parents, that would be a red flag for me.

Finally, family members (and usually even kindergarten children) feel "good" or "bad" about a school, and should discuss their feelings—their reactions to the people, the environment, the pedagogical approach, and other criteria that are important. After careful deliberation, with an eye toward their child's needs and their family's values, parents can make a more informed decision.

Our son has Attention Deficit Disorder. The public schools in our neighborhood couldn't accommodate his needs.

Chet, father of Roger, 8

Parent Conferences

- -

"When we had our first parent conference, I was quite anxious," said Margaret. "Billy is our only child and I was worried because his transition to kindergarten had not been easy. I wondered whether his adjustment difficulties would affect his performance."

"He was doing fine," countered Margaret's husband, Joe. "He had stopped crying when I dropped him off in the morning and had made a bunch of friends."

Margaret shrugged her shoulders, confirming that she and her husband viewed the situation differently. "In anticipation of our conference, I jotted down a few questions."

"Fifteen to be exact," Joe volunteered, with a slight smile on his face.

"Okay, well you must have realized by now, I am anal retentive and slightly neurotic," she said with a laugh, which broke the tension in the room. "I may have gone a bit overboard."

"A bit?" Joe asked. "Picture this. We walk into this kindergarten classroom that has been transformed into an aquarium because the kids are studying ocean mammals. The teacher, Mr. McCormick, who has taught for ten years, greets us and invites us to sit down. On the desk in front of him is a folder with Billy's name on it. Before he can begin speaking, Margaret takes her two-page list of questions out of her leather portfolio and looks like she is going to begin reading it aloud."

"Okay, so it was a slightly aggressive move," Margaret concurred.

"Before Margaret can speak, the teacher tells us what a great kid Billy is. He's smart but impatient, bossy, and he's got a short fuse. But he apologizes when he's wrong, and together they are working on his 'impulse control issues.' When I was a kid they called it hitting," Joe said.

"Mr. McCormick also observed that Billy is intelligent. He has excellent leadership skills and the other children like him," Margaret interjected.

"He was right on target," Joe said.

"So what happened to your list of questions?" I asked Margaret.

Her face slightly flushed.

"I put them back in her portfolio," Joe intervened. "Our time was up. Besides, I was sure Margaret wouldn't press the man after he'd done such a good job."

"Absolutely, darling," Margaret agreed.

The Parent-Teacher Team

Marie Hedley Rush teaches kindergarten at Alimacani Elementary School in Jacksonville, Florida.

The first few months of kindergarten are stressful for most parents. The initial parent conference may be even more so. As your child's first teacher, you probably have a pretty good idea how your child is doing overall. The parent conference is an opportunity to learn how your child is faring in the classroom environment where there are new and different anxieties, as well as challenges.

*Our parent conference
with Justin's teacher
was quite odd. I was
prepared to talk about
academics, and she talked
about motor skills.*

John, father of
Justin, 8

From the beginning of school on, it is important to realize that you and your child's teacher are a team. It is your responsibility to make sure that he or she has been updated on all medical, social, and emotional issues. Don't be afraid to phone, send an E-mail, or write a note. It's important that your child's teacher understands information about your son or daughter that may be affecting classroom behavior. A difficult developmental period, new sibling, or family illness can be significant influences.

If there is a problem, and a note won't do, feel free to request a parent conference. Don't feel you must wait until the teacher requests one. Before the conference, it is always a good idea to jot down your questions and concerns. That way when you meet with your child's teacher, you will be able to remember the issues you would like to discuss. You should realize, however, that in many schools, the formal conferences may be scheduled back to back, and there might be a limited period of time.

In these formal conferences, teachers usually begin by telling parents how the children are doing. Are they comfortable in the classroom setting? Are they beginning to understand the basic routines? Are they playing with the other children in a constructive manner? Do they participate in class discussions? Can they describe their feelings? How are they handling conflict resolution? Are they able to use words to solve problems or is impulse control (usually hitting and/or kicking) a problem?

The teacher will also show you samples of your child's work that have been set aside for the conference. You'll see pictures your child has drawn, samples of numbers and letters he or she has written, perhaps some pages in his or her journal, and other projects that may be reflective of your child's abilities.

In anticipation of the conference, you should recognize that your child's teacher may also wish to discuss the areas in which your child needs improvement. Constructive criticism should be presented in a helpful manner. It's important that when your child's teacher discusses problems, he or she also suggests potential solutions. The best teachers will include you in that discussion.

At best, a parent conference presents an opportunity for you and your child's teacher to exchange information. It is an opportunity for the teacher to share his or her thoughts and for you to share yours. It should be a venue for you to express your concerns as well as to discuss the "good stuff." And if you haven't already done so, the parent conference is a good avenue to learn how you may participate more fully in your child's education, either in school or at home.

Developing a relationship with your child's teacher is a key element of a successful educational experience. The better you, your spouse, your child, and his or her teacher can communicate, the more satisfying everyone's experience will be.

My daughter's major problem was socialization. Her teacher worked with my wife and me so that we could reinforce at home what she was doing at school.

Connor, father of
Melanie, 6, and
Robby, 9

Parental Involvement

"When our daughter Lisa started kindergarten," Christina said, "she brought home a list of volunteer opportunities that was ten pages long. My husband Luis and I could help in the kindergarten classroom, become room representatives, drive on field trips, serve on PTA committees, volunteer to tutor other children, participate in fund-raising activities, help out in the library or in the school office, work at school cleanup day, and help in dozens of other ways.

"Upon looking at the list, Luis jokingly said, 'Why can't we just give money?' When Martin, our fourteen-year-old son, was in school Luis was asked to do nothing except drive him there.

"'Different time, different schools,' I told him, and then I asked whether I should sign him up for the fund-raising committee, the yearly auction, or cleanup day. 'Show me the money,' he said. 'I'll be on the fund-raising committee. What are you going to sign up for?'

"I told him that to start with I was going to work in Lisa's classroom one day a week and drive carpools on field trips.

"'Sounds good,' he said.

"I can't tell you how great this entire experience has been," Christina said to me. "I am so pleased we have the opportunity to play such an active role in Lisa's school. Volunteering in her kindergarten class was wonderful. Not only did I develop a relationship with her teacher, but I could also see which kids she played with, arrange play dates, and meet a lot of other mothers. The field trips were really fun.

"After his first year on the fund-raising committee, Luis volunteered to chair it. The next year the committee raised $50,000—double what they'd gotten the previous year. Luis works in marketing and he had some great ideas. The parents on his committee were receptive and hard workers.

"Since our state ranks in the middle range in the country on educational funding per child, the money we've contributed is paying for wonderful things, like more school aides, computers, and a part-time art teacher.

"What's interesting is that we're not a wealthy school. Most of the parents are middle class, with some discretionary income. But educating our children is our first priority. I've never volunteered for anything that has given me such satisfaction.

"When I walk Lisa to school each morning and see so many parents I know, I finally feel we're part of a wonderful community."

I work full-time, so I can't volunteer in the classroom. But I take time off to drive on field trips, and that makes my son so happy.

Liz, mother of
Darth, 6

Parents and Teachers as Partners

Natalie Thomas has been an elementary school teacher for fifteen years. She teaches at George H. Conley Elementary School in Rosindale, Massachusetts.

Long before your children enter kindergarten, you, the parents, are their first teachers. You talk to them so that they hear words and learn to communicate. You read to them so that they develop a love of books. You nurture them so that they feel good about themselves. You praise them so that their accomplishments—big or small—help them feel capable and competent. It is this kind of support that enables children to feel confident as they encounter new experiences.

As your children enter kindergarten, once again your attitude will affect theirs. Your willingness to participate in their classroom and in school activities is a sign that you care. Your enthusiasm for their school experience will provide a model for their feelings. Simply put, if you are happy, they will be happy. And one of the best ways to do this is to open the lines of communication and develop a partnership with your child's teacher. Partnerships always involve a give-and-take relationship. The following are some recommendations on how this might work out.

Volunteering is a wonderful experience. At our school, kindergarten is the only time when you can work in the classroom on a regular basis. It's also been a great way to meet new friends.

Tama, mother of
Stacy, 5

TEACHERS AS PARTNERS

- Before school starts, provide an orientation program for parents and children that introduces them to the world of kindergarten.
- Upon registration, present parents with information outlining your goals and addressing their expectations.
- Send letters home as a means of communication.
- Arrange for home visits, phone conferences, classroom visits, and parent conferences.
- Prepare an informational presentation for the Open House.
- Comment on student work.
- Use bulletin boards to communicate information that is relevant to parents' concerns and needs.
- Use bulletin boards to display children's work.

PARENTS AS PARTNERS

- Become a room representative; assist with the phone network.

- Fill out the classroom survey of ways you might be able to participate in class—talents you have or resources you can offer.
- Drive on field trips.
- Read books in class.
- Help with one-on-one tutoring; participate in small-group teaching.
- Assist with clerical or housekeeping jobs.
- Share cooking expertise; help during snack time.
- Make costumes.
- Participate in multicultural activities, birthday parties, and holiday celebrations.

I work at home, so I have the freedom to participate during the day. Our school is very small. There is a high expectation that parents should volunteer. Because we don't have a school cafeteria, we provide hot lunches four days a week.

Sandra, mother of
Donny, 17 months,
and Suzi, 6

Parents Helping Kids Learn

Shelly Quinn teaches kindergarten at Home Elementary School in Stickney, Illinois.

To keep parents informed, I send a newsletter home each Friday that outlines our activities for the week. In this newsletter I list things parents can send in for certain activities (this helps working moms in particular feel like they are contributing). As part of our daily routine, I welcome parent volunteers to come in and work with small groups of children. Parents can read stories or observe their child teaching the calendar. I do not, however, encourage parents to just pop in at any time as this can be rather disruptive. Sometimes a child will act up more if his or her parent is in the classroom, so obviously this is not a good situation either. I have also sent games and other projects to be made at home by parent volunteers—working moms love this too.

When parents are actively involved in the classroom, it can allow the teacher more small group opportunities without interruption. It is wonderful for the kids to have another adult to go to. Children feel a great sense of pride when their parents come to help out in the room or on a field trip. The only time I discourage parental involvement in the classroom is when a child is too clingy and the adult pays attention to only her or his child.

One of the simplest things parents can do is to check their child's backpack on a daily basis. I have found weeks' worth of notes, papers, newsletters, etc., in a child's backpack. Support what your child does, take an interest in his or her schoolwork. I also encourage parents to use my newsletter as a conversation starter about their child's days at school. I think a good "come home" routine is important. There needs to be time each day to look through backpacks, do homework, discuss any notes from the teacher or the school. One of the most important ways parents can enable their child to succeed in school is to get to know and support the teacher. Letting children watch a TV show in which kids act naughty when they've had behavior issues at school sends a mixed message to the children.

Parental involvement usually goes hand in hand with appropriate school behavior. Parents who believe school is important instill that belief in their child. As a result, attendance and performance are better. The key to success in the classroom is follow-through at home. This follow-through can include positive reinforcement as well as the recognition of possible behavior problems.

One of the hardest adjustments for parents of kindergartners is to let go just a little bit more when they send their children off. That big break from parents is a milestone in a child's life. Often it is harder on the parent than it is on the child. Kindergarten is a big step in the direction of independence and self-confidence and should be treated in a positive, cheerful manner.

As a single father, it was a problem. I volunteered to be a room representative, but none of the mothers ever called me or asked me to participate in the phone tree. When the teacher intervened, everything changed.

Paul, father of
Meredith, 6, and
Brittany, 8

Physical Education

- -

A few years ago, when I was shopping at my neighborhood mall, I ran into Liz, a woman with whom I'd gone through elementary school. We hadn't seen each other for years. So we each bought a cup of coffee, sat down, and caught up on our lives. Suddenly, out of the blue, Liz said, "You know, I really want to thank you for always choosing me to be on your team."

"What team?" I asked, genuinely surprised.

"Primarily sockball and kickball," she responded somewhat seriously. "You and Betty Ann were always voted captains, and you consistently chose me first."

I laughed aloud. "Liz, you've gotta be kidding. That was decades ago. It's still memorable?" I asked, with shock registering on my face.

"You've got a child; you should know."

"What do you mean?"

"My two older daughters are terrific athletes. My five-year-old Molly is not. From the time she was a toddler, I took her to a variety of Mommy and Me classes in swimming, movement, and play. She hated them all so we quit. Later the girls tried to teach her how to catch and kick a ball, run, and hop. She showed no interest in learning. They never pushed."

For a half hour each week, we have a PE coach who teaches the children games, rules, and sportsmanship. On a regular basis, the teachers supervise outdoor play, and the kids mostly play with balls.

Clark, father of
Cameron, 6

147

The teachers take the children out to the big yard once a week and teach them how to skip rope and hop. They even teach them jumping jacks. There's a basketball hoop in the kindergarten yard, but it's mainly the boys who use it.

Louise, mother
of Riva, 6,
Hadassah, 9, and
Rebecca, 10

"Why all the emphasis on sports?" I asked.

"My husband, Greg, who's not athletic and knows how that made him feel throughout school, feels physical education is very important. He doesn't care if Molly is only an average athlete, but he wants her to be good enough to be able to play with the other children. He wasn't, and it took its toll."

"Isn't she learning new skills in kindergarten?" I asked.

"No," Liz shook her head. "When she started, I told her teacher she needed help in this area. Mrs. Duncan said that one-on-one teaching is reserved for academic problems. She suggested we talk to the principal. So Greg and I met with the principal and talked about the importance of a progressive skill-building program where children's abilities and skills are adequately assessed. The principal agreed but said physical education is an 'extra.' Schools decide how to budget their money, and Molly's school uses these funds for computers. There was nothing more for us to say."

"Maybe she'll get better as she matures," I suggested.

"You know that when kids don't start out as athletes they rarely improve. Besides, Molly's such a perfectionist. She won't participate in something in which she doesn't excel."

I didn't know how to respond. There was a moment of uncomfortable silence until Liz smiled and said, "Sorry, these feelings have been building up for a while. I guess when I saw you, I realized how grateful I was that you were there for me."

"That's all right," I responded. "I never knew what a big deal it had been. I wonder what happened to the kids Betty Ann and I picked last."

"You mean Alice and Gail?"

We both laughed because we vividly remembered those names as if it were yesterday.

"I've heard that Alice still lives with her parents," Liz said.

"Oh God," I said, feeling a surge of guilt. "And Gail?" I hesitated to ask.

"She's a brain surgeon in New York."

My guilt dissipated within moments. We gossiped about everyone else we remembered, and then said good-bye.

Movement Programs for Children

Steve Saunders, Ph.D., is a professor in the Department of Human Movement Studies at the University of Memphis, Tennessee.

Parents seeking information about their children's kindergarten experiences should not forget to ask about physical education. Physical activity plays a very important part in each child's overall development. After all, children learn by moving through their environment. A quality physical education program for kindergarten children provides developmentally appropriate practice, as defined by the Council on Physical Education for Children (COPEC), the nation's largest professional association of children's physical education teachers. The COPEC position is that quality daily physical education should be available to all children. There should be a recognition that each child will have a different background in terms of previous movement experiences, fitness and skill levels, body size, and age. The best programs encompass four primary components.

■ **Developing psychomotor skills.** Physical education teachers should develop activities that assist children in developing locomotor, nonmanipulative, and manipulative skills. Locomotor skills include walking, running, hopping, chasing, fleeing, and dodging. Nonmanipulative skills encompass turning, twisting, balancing, and transferring weight. Manipulative skills include throwing, catching, dribbling, kicking, and hitting with a racquet.

■ **Actively involving every child.** Each and every child should be allowed to participate in physical education programs. Years ago, it was thought that young children would develop skills and knowledge about skills by participating in activities such as relays or playing games such as "Duck, Duck,

My oldest child is mainstreamed but has special needs. Her physical therapist is quite wonderful. My youngest daughter is just uncoordinated. She never progressed at all.

Elsie, mother of
Lory, 5, and
Julie, 7

Goose." Today we know that in order to develop skills, children need to be active. Games and activities that force children to waste time sitting and/or waiting for a turn to participate do not provide children with the time needed to develop skills. It's important that all children have ample practice time. There should be no lines, plenty of equipment, and no activities that eliminate children from games.

■ **Promoting success.** Participating in activities that provide for success is another important criterion. Activities that are too difficult may discourage child participation. Children may become frustrated and stop practicing skills. Activities that are too easy may turn children off to physical activity as well. Research suggests that activities should be planned so that children are successful about 70 to 80 percent of the time.

■ **Providing proper equipment.** Proper equipment is key in helping children develop skills. We would not expect classroom teachers to provide one crayon or one pair of scissors for an entire class. We should not ask physical education teachers to do this either.

What is important for parents to remember is that physical activity is crucial to a child's development. In addition, the kindergarten year is considered the fundamental stage of development, a period of skill development that has a significant influence on establishing a positive attitude and appreciation for a lifetime of participation in regular health-related physical activity.

Learning about letters, numbers, colors, and shapes are all important for children, but don't forget that movement skills are equally important.

When I was a child, we played in the yard, and it wasn't even a special one for kindergarten kids. Now there is all this emphasis on developing motor skills. At first I thought they were teaching the kids to drive.

Robert, father of Emma, 7, and Brent, 9

Play

"How important do you think play is in kindergarten?" I asked Bernie one weekend when he was in his studio painting a watercolor landscape. He didn't answer right away, so I assumed it was because he hadn't heard me. Vivaldi was cranked up high on his stereo and he seemed lost in thought.

I loudly cleared my voice. "Bernie," I said, repeating myself, "how important do you think . . . ?"

Before I could finish, he walked over to the stereo, turned down the volume, and walked back to his chair so that he faced me. He looked me in the eyes and said with some annoyance at having been disturbed, "Very!"

"Do you have any particular feelings about free play, directed play, guided play, dramatic play, and outdoor play?" I asked with enthusiasm, ignoring his obvious disinterest.

He grunted. After a pause, he said with some concern, "You know, you should probably take a day off. Rest and read."

"Why?" I asked, with genuine surprise.

"Honey, play is play! I think this is getting more complex than it need be."

My wife told me that play is a method of expression, a way for children to learn and to relate to others. When I took a day off from work to help in the classroom, all I saw was the kids throwing Legos at each other.

Booth, father of
Kenyon, 5, and
Wade, 7

A*s a middle-school teacher, I know that children learn through play. I'm sorry that the elementary school curriculum is becoming more oriented toward academics, not play.*

Marjorie, mother
of Brendon, 6, and
Johnny, 11.

"No, listen for a minute," I earnestly replied. "I used to think that play is play, but it's really not. As Friedrich Froebel, who is pretty much credited for developing the concept of kindergarten, said, 'Play is the purest, most spiritual activity of man at this stage, and at the same time, typical of human life as a whole, of the inner hidden natural life in man and all things. It gives, therefore, joy, freedom, contentment, inner and outer rest, peace with the world.'"

Bernie looked at me in a quizzical way, but it didn't dissuade me from continuing my monologue. "There are important differences among types of play," I continued without a breath. "You see, I just read this book, *Joyful Learning in Kindergarten,* in which the author, Bobbi Fisher, quantifies plays. She talks about 'free' play, which is just that; children are free to pick the materials with which they want to play."

He closed his eyes for a moment and probably would have covered his ears with his hands if it hadn't been such a childlike response. Of course I was undeterred and continued with the enthusiasm of a TV evangelist. "'Directed' play, be it individualized or cooperative, is more focused and is facilitated by the teacher."

Even though Bernie's eyes now had glazed over, I was on a roll and continued with enthusiasm. "The teacher directs 'guided' play, which is orchestrated toward fulfilling specific objectives."

Obviously trying to cut off this conversation before it went a moment further, Bernie said, "I'm assuming that dramatic play encourages expression of emotions and outdoor play allows the children to smell the flowers, so to speak."

"Precisely," I said with an encouraging smile.

He paused. "Do you think that perhaps you are obsessing about the concept of play?"

"Absolutely not!" I responded with irritation.

"When Alex was in kindergarten, what kind of play did he engage in?" Bernie asked.

"I have no idea. Who knew there were so many different categories of play?"

"When you were a kid, how and where did you play?" he asked.

"Outdoors. But obviously a lot of research on play has been done since then."

"When I was a kid we played indoors in the winter because it snowed. We played outdoors in the spring, summer, and fall because the weather was better. We swam at a public pool, played Kick the Can, rode our bikes, walked around our neighborhood, and tossed a ball."

"Oh, honey," I said in what I hoped was not a discouraging tone. "I'm afraid you're talking about the acquisition of motor skills rather than play."

He shook his head, looked at me as if I were an alien, turned on the Vivaldi CD, and once again sat in his chair facing his painting.

"Well!" I said in a huff as I marched off to shoot some hoops with Alex, who had been much more receptive when I had given him a mini-lecture on the same subject.

Once he had sunk a few shots, he turned to me and said, "This outdoor motor development activity is fun; almost feels like play."

I patted his head and smiled. At least someone understood me.

> *The kids play at home. They should learn at school.*
>
> Deborah, mother of Roger, 6, and Ethan, 8

Learning Through Play

Jerome L. Singer, Ph.D., is a professor of psychology at Yale University and codirector of the Yale University Family Television Research and Consultation Center. He is also the author, with his wife Dorothy G. Singer, Ph.D., of *The House of Make-Believe: Children's Play and the Developing Imagination.*

Why is it so important that kindergarten children play?

There are different kinds of play, and each one has benefits for children. Physical play or sensorimotor play where children practice skills and movement improves their agility

There are more impor-
tant issues in life than
whether our kindergartners
play too much or too little
in school, don't you
think?

Joan, mother of
Patrick, 7

and mobility. It is fun to do and an important part of the whole growth process.

Another kind of play is make-believe, pretending or symbolic play, where kids make up stories and act out adventures and plots. Make-believe play begins at about age two-and-a-half or three and runs through age six before children tend to inhibit it. As children grow, pretend play becomes the foundation for the inner resources of imagination that every adult requires. Imaginative play is associated with trying out new roles, new ways of behaving in relation to others, and ways of resolving problems. Children practice new concepts and vocabulary through play. It also improves skills, such as counting. Most important, all our research shows that play is fun. It makes children happy. They have carved a piece out of the big outside world and put it under their control in miniature form.

Imaginative play reaches its peak in the period between four and five years of age. While it doesn't disappear completely, children learn that it is not acceptable behavior to say all their thoughts out loud. They have to learn to restrain themselves so that pretend play becomes internalized in the form of their inner imagination. We know that children who play more imaginatively are also likely to be somewhat more creative, and they are better behaved. They are also less likely to be aggressive.

Kids who are aggressive usually start out with the idea of playing but pretty quickly start hitting other kids. Kids who play imaginatively and have been encouraged to do this by family are more likely to work out problems in the plots of their stories and less likely to hurt other kids. They are also more cooperative with each other in order to keep the game going. They have to take different parts. Sometimes they are the hero and other times the villain.

Another form of play introduced around this time is games, such as board games, with definite rules. These games teach children restraint, self-discipline, and the importance of taking turns, skills that are the beginnings of citizenship. Games with rules are important and often can be combined with make-believe story plots. That way children can get the benefits of both kinds of play.

What effect is the push toward academics having on play?

I have no objection to the push toward academics to some degree, but I think the way that children really will make better progress is if the academics are worked into game behavior. Otherwise, learning is boring and they are not motivated to sustain it. If you put new concepts into story form or little playlets, children get excited. They like the idea of acting out the story, and the teacher can still work in new vocabulary and concepts. The key is to try to keep the game fun for the kids.

What kinds of play should parents encourage?

The foundation of building an active imagination has to start before kindergarten. Imagination begins with parents who talk to their children. There is substantial research that shows there are parents who hardly talk to their kids other than to give them orders or yell at them. As early as possible, parents need to talk to their children, explain things to them, tell them stories and read to them at bedtime. You create in children a readiness for imaginative play by telling them stories and encouraging them to talk and explore. Parents should actually get down on the floor and start a make-believe game with their children. Children really need that initial push, but then once they've done it a couple of times they really don't want the parents involved in their play. They want to take it over themselves.

I don't know one adult who wouldn't like some playtime scheduled in his or her workday.

> Bruce, father of
> Shannon, 4,
> Megan, 6, and
> Jonathan, 10

Play in My Kindergarten Class

Jack Fontanella teaches kindergarten at Harborview Elementary School in Juneau, Alaska.

Play in kindergarten is everything and everything is play. Play is how five- and six-year-old children relate to the world. Through play we learn so many things. We learn to be social, that is, we learn how to make friends and how to negotiate so that we can keep friends. We figure out our place in the world through play, and act out present and future roles to help us practice and learn important skills. We develop our future pathways in our brains through our play in early childhood. So how does this relate to my kindergarten classroom?

In my classroom, play is imbedded in the program all through the school day. We start our day with play. Much of my math program is delivered through games. We practice writing through play throughout the day. We may need to make a sign for our "store," or to write a *save* sign for a block building. We may be taking orders for our "restaurant." Or we may be making a list of all those who want to come to our birthday party in March when it is now October. Even in reading, at this time of year we "play read." We read the pictures and make up the words, or we repeat what we remember of the story as we look at the pictures. We play at educational computer games. We play, play, play all day, and we learn.

As I have already stated, we start our day with play, that is, we have our *developmental centers* time first thing in the morning. What we call *developmental centers* others call *choice time* or *free play,* and free-choice playtime is exactly what it is. Playtime is an important part of the day in most early childhood classrooms, but in many of these classes, it is left for the end of the day. I would like to make a case for putting playtime first thing in the morning. As my children come into the room they turn their attendance cards around to the *I am here* side, hang up their coats and put their lunches and other personal gear in their cubbies, check in last night's read-aloud book and check out a new book with me, and go straight to playing with friends. There is stuff set out on the tables, play dough, and a theme-related art activity or two. Parents are here to help out at the centers and just to help us start our day. The whole room is open and we can play with

Play is what kindergarten is all about.

Amy, mother of
Melody, 3, and
Elliott, 5

anything we like. The play is calm and focused, and the noise level is a soft murmur, most days. Compare this to free time at the end of the day when everyone is at least a little tired, and maybe a little grumpy. The noise level is usually fairly high, and if you look closely you might see quite a lot of unfocused wandering. And why not start out the day with the children's favorite activity? What a great thing to look forward to every morning!

Principals

Before Alex started elementary school, I never fully understood the role of the principal. I can remember the name of every single grade school teacher I had when I was a kid, but I have no idea who the principal was. Neither does my childhood friend Melissa. She says it's because the only children who knew the principal were the troublemakers.

"If only we could find Bobby, Ronnie, Mitch, or Lorraine [four of the ringleaders in our class], we'd find out her name," Melissa suggested.

I laughed. "I wonder if they still get in trouble all the time."

"Who knows? They certainly got a lot of individual attention in elementary school. Think of it. They must have seen the principal on a weekly basis, and we can't remember her name."

"I always thought her name was 'The Principal,'" I jokingly said. "The only time we ever heard about her was when a teacher said, 'If you do that one more time, I'll send you to The Principal.'"

We both laughed again. The reason Melissa and I were even discussing the subject was that I wondered what role the principal of Alex's school would play in his life, and ours. Bernie and my friends who had elementary-school children said the principal (in this case, a woman) is like the president. The values she promotes, by her actions as well as her words, set the entire tone of the school. The essence of her very being—who she is, what she cares about, what her priorities are, the criteria she uses to hire new teachers, and what her expectations are of the children, the teachers, and the parents—will make or break the school.

On the night of the school roundup when our principal had first spoken to prospective parents, she had been impressive. On the first day of school, she was articulate, authoritative (without being imperious), coolheaded, and understanding. She also demonstrated her quick wit, which of course made all the difference to me.

In the weeks and months that followed, I slowly began to understand the breadth and depth of her job. I had immediately recognized her personal qualities that made us all feel so good about our school, and reassured that our children were well taken care of. She was visible, accessible, and friendly. She learned our names and those of our children. With seven hundred families, that's no small accomplishment.

She held parenting sessions for all grade levels where she addressed parental fears, neuroses, and anxieties. We saw her in the classrooms and on the playground. She attended all school events, chaired the school-based management meetings (ours is a charter school that is run by the principal, teachers, and parents), and most important, she was always available to talk with parents and their children.

This is some of what we saw. We knew she wore many other hats; she was a mentor to teachers, our school's representative to the district, and a curricular innovator. She was the proponent of, and administrative role model for, a new kind of educational system—one that works.

Six years later, when I cried at Alex's elementary school graduation, I wasn't sure whether it was because I was so

It seems to me that in the best schools, the teachers and principals are a strong team.

Darcy, mother of
Rueben, 8, and
Preston, 11

proud of him (and I was), or because I understood how sorely I'd miss our principal.

In fact, it was both.

The Role of the Principal

Vincent L. Ferrandino, Ph.D., is the executive director of the National Association of Elementary School Principals.

What impact does the principal have on an elementary school?

The principal oversees all aspects of the elementary school, providing instructional leadership for the teachers as well as working with the community and especially with the parents to provide a safe, effective learning environment. The type of leadership provided by the principal creates the overall environment within which the students and teachers live while at school.

What is the essence of the principal's job?

The main focus of the principal's job is to be certain that an environment is created within the school that is welcoming and nurturing to young people and supportive of the teachers and staff. He or she creates an environment where students can learn and achieve at high levels and at the same time feel comfortable and safe. The principal also creates a supportive environment and builds the foundation for a partnership with parents. For example, the transition to kindergarten is traumatic for parents, especially if it is the first time they send a child off to school. Principals are aware of the trauma involved and will do all they can to ease the situation. I can remember very clearly the first time we sent our first one off. You have all kinds of thoughts running through your head: Is this the right place for him? We've done so much to try to create a loving, caring environment. Is the school going to be that for him? All those issues are important. The principal is there to help the parent through that process.

What is the principal's relationship with the children, the teachers, and the parents?

The principal has a unique relationship with each of these groups. For the children, the principal serves as the one who cares for their overall well-being during the school day. He or she is viewed as a surrogate parent while the student is there. The principal is the person children can look to for help and support if they are having any difficulties with their classroom situation.

For the teachers, the principal is there to give guidance, to offer support for their instructional work, and to make sure that they have the necessary resources to carry on their responsibilities.

For the parents, the principal is one of the key communicators between the school and the home. Parents ought to look to the principal as someone they can go to with any issue that is related to school, as well as inform the principal of any issues that are taking place at home that may impact the student's performance. And likewise, the principal has a responsibility to inform the parents of any issues that are taking place at the school that might inhibit the student from performing to his or her fullest potential.

What are the qualities of an outstanding principal?

First of all, the principal needs to be someone who truly loves children, understands the needs of children of the various age levels within the school, and understands how children learn and how they grow. The principal needs to be a person who communicates effectively with children and parents. He or she should provide leadership to the teachers by providing them with instructional leadership as well as with leadership around the organization of the school day and the various activities that take place within the school.

Do you think the quality of the principal can affect the overall quality of the school?

I don't think there is any question about that. In my job as director of the National Association of Elementary School Principals, I have visited numerous effective schools and I have never seen one outstanding school where there was not an outstanding principal present.

Being Principal

Barbara Wong taught kindergarten for nine years. She has been a principal for thirteen years, two of them at Park City School in Alhambra, California.

Our principal strongly supports his teachers. Whenever there's a problem, he requests that the parents talk to the teacher. He only intervenes when it's not resolved.

Janie, mother of Benjamin, 7

A principal's responsibilities seemingly include everything under the sun, and according to my job description, "other duties as assigned." Thus, I am an instructional leader, disciplinarian, problem solver, negotiator, visionary, mentor to teachers, counselor, juggler (balancing the micro with the macro), crisis manager, restroom supervisor, food service overseer, fund-raiser, cheerleader, chaperone, night supervisor, bus driver, evaluator, and campus security person and plant manager.

I am also the liaison to the PTA and school site council. I participate in school activities, teach parent education activities, and attend local and regional meetings and conferences. I work in the classrooms with students, read to them, develop curriculum for them, resolve conflicts between them, and help enhance their academic achievement.

My mission is to implement programs that create a positive and productive learning environment that celebrates achievement and fosters creative and effective pedagogical practices. Having been a teacher for fifteen years, nine as a kindergarten teacher, I feel that I have a good and realistic sense of life and its challenges in the classroom. I have a good understanding of the needs of the teachers and the students.

From my ten years as an administrator, I have learned I would be an even better teacher now, because of the opportunity to observe some very talented educators effectively implement outstanding teaching practices and strategies.

One of the greatest challenges I have is to be a change agent, responsible for implementing effective educational reform while dancing on a shifting carpet and feeling like a member of Cirque du Soleil. It is also a challenge to be positive and hopeful in the face of constant criticism from the public and the mass media. But I am a child of the sixties, so I gotta have hope! Every day is a new day, a new challenge. The kids are the reason I trek across town every day—and despite all the problems, they are learning and good stuff is going on in those classrooms.

We had a weak principal but strong teachers and involved parents. There wasn't a dramatic change for the better until the principal retired.

Evelyn, mother of
Kimberly, 8, and
Traci, 14

Public Schools

At the beginning of Alex's last year of preschool, a half-dozen mothers must have asked me where he was going to kindergarten. I said I didn't know.

"Haven't you been visiting schools?" Lucy, a particularly aggressive mom, asked.

"Nope," I replied.

"Why not?"

"Because I'm not ready to think about it. Who knows what Alex will be like in another year? Besides, we have a great public school in our neighborhood."

"But if you want him to go to private school, you must begin applying right away," she said.

"But I don't want him to go to private school," I answered. "Bernie and I both went to public school. Philosophically, I believe in public education."

She walked away. Obviously I was no longer worth talking to.

Six months later, Bernie and I attended the school roundup, an evening meeting for prospective parents at our local elementary school. The auditorium was packed. As we sat in our chairs, the tension in the room was palpable.

The principal was reassuring. I breathed a sigh of relief. She explained that while our school was a public school, it was also a charter school. At that time there were only one hundred charter schools in the country. The advantage was that while we were part of our school district, the principal and teachers had far more freedom to determine the school's mission, goals, objectives, and curriculum. The kindergarten teachers who spoke were enthusiastic and articulate. The parents were actively involved in school-based management. Bernie and I felt so lucky.

Right after the meeting I went up to one of the teachers and rather nervously said, "It takes my son a while to adjust to new situations. He tends to start out as an observer rather than a participant. Will that be a problem?"

"No," she said, with a warm and gentle voice. "Our expectation is that every child is unique. While there may be certain developmental similarities, their personalities, learning styles, backgrounds, motor skill development, and social and intellectual skills differ. It is a wonderful challenge to figure out what is the best way to teach each child so he or she can flourish."

I was so relieved I almost wept. Bernie smiled, thanked the teacher for her time, and started walking away. I pulled him back and said, "I have one more question."

Bernie looked at me with an expression that said "Enough is enough. Let her talk to the ten other couples who are standing behind us in line." Completely ignoring him, I quietly said, "Alex is our only child. Is this a loving environment?"

She smiled, patted my shoulder, and said, "Of course, and it's a wonderful school. Don't worry."

I profusely thanked her and Bernie and I left the auditorium. When we were outside he shook his head, turned to me, raised his eyebrows, and said, "Is this a loving environment? Honey, what was she going to say? 'No, the teachers here hate kids.'"

"It wasn't what she said," I explained. "It was the look on her face when she said it."

The public school in our neighborhood was horrible, so I had to look around. We found a great private school we couldn't afford. We found another public school we really liked in a different neighborhood. We moved.

Miguel, father of Paolo, 5

"Golly neds," he replied, which is his peculiar expression when he thinks I'm wacko.

I took his arm, sighed once more, and walked into the night knowing Alex would be in good hands.

The Public Venue

Patricia Reeves is a kindergarten teacher and chair of the Early Childhood Educator's Caucus of the National Education Association.

Why should children attend public schools?

I'm biased because I'm a public school teacher. But I am also a mother who had to determine the best learning environment for my own children. I chose to send them to public school then, and I would make the same choice today. Our society is diverse, and learning encompasses more than reading, writing, and arithmetic. We need to provide an environment where our children can become playmates and friends with other children from different ethnic, socioeconomic, and cultural backgrounds. I believe public school offers us an unparalleled opportunity.

What are the notable recent achievements in kindergarten education?

The first is an increased access, for almost all children, to attend kindergarten programs. Although kindergarten is not mandatory in every state, there is indisputable evidence affirming its value for all children. Teachers and other experts know that effective kindergarten programs enable children to develop the interpersonal, academic, and socialization skills that provide a strong foundation for future educational success.

Research confirms that full-day kindergarten, a fairly recent innovation, is particularly beneficial to children who do not come from nurturing homes. Although many pre-schools and Head Start programs are providing some of the basic skills, kindergarten gives these children a chance to catch up with their peers. Statistics also confirm that an increasing number of dual-income families strongly favor an extended kindergarten program with a strong developmentally appropriate curriculum, staffed by qualified professionals.

A third achievement is an increased willingness to consider combining effective teaching methodologies rather than pitting them against each other. Since there is overall recognition that children learn in different ways, it only makes sense to provide different learning opportunities. This is particularly evident in teaching literacy. The combination of phonics (a method of teaching where letters represent sounds and there is an emphasis on word recognition) and the whole language approach (in which listening, speaking, reading, and writing are combined) provides children with more opportunities to be successful.

Another important improvement is the increased availability of hands-on materials for teaching math and science. It has long been known that children learn more effectively when they are able to use concrete materials. Manipulatives—such as pattern blocks, wooden cubes, linking blocks (Multi-links, Unifix cubes), and Geoboards—have always been important learning tools. In the past, many school administrators did not provide sufficient funds for these items, perhaps because they did not recognize their importance. Priorities have changed in this area.

What is the state of kindergarten education in the United States?

There are a lot of excellent kindergarten programs throughout the country and always have been. A critical problem is one of consistency; many states still do not have mandatory kindergarten. In a National Education Association survey on the state of kindergarten in the United States, the results confirmed each state has different regulations for class size, length of day, cutoff date for beginning school, and testing. The research on the importance of funding more programs for younger children has resulted in increased federal funding in this area, but there still are a number of issues that need to be addressed, including the following:

We're lucky because our neighborhood school is good, and the parents have a strong voice. There is a great opportunity for involvement, and you can work in your child's classroom.

Taki, mother of
Hana, 7

■ **Class size.** It varies from state to state. In some school districts there may be ten to twelve children in one class; in another, twenty to thirty. Some kindergarten teachers are responsible for teaching two half-day sessions, with a total enrollment of forty to sixty children. Obviously those teachers do not have time to develop personal relationships with all the children in their classes and their families. An important goal is to reduce class size.

■ **Full-day kindergarten.** As I mentioned earlier, the availability of full-day kindergarten programs is increasing. While this seems to be a positive step forward because it allows both children and teachers to get to know each other better and to spend more time on activities, it will be important to see the results of longitudinal studies.

■ **Assessment.** While the alleged purpose of standardized testing is to provide a method for evaluating children on a nationwide basis, many teachers and other educational experts believe this type of testing is not developmentally appropriate for kindergarten children; there are far better ways of evaluating children's progress. Another critical concern is that there is an increasing emphasis on preparing children for testing rather than on educating them.

■ **Cutoff dates.** With more families moving from state to state, there is a growing need to create a universal policy regarding cutoff dates for beginning school. As children enter schools in different geographic areas, their parents are finding their children may have to wait an additional year to qualify for entrance into kindergarten or begin kindergarten a year earlier. In either case, the age ranges in classrooms are increasing, thrusting children of many different developmental stages into one class.

While we might conclude that public kindergarten education is in a state of flux, it is promising to note the spreading awareness of the importance of early childhood education. As I have become active in the National Education Association and have met other kindergarten teachers throughout the country, I am gratified to see their commitment to teaching all children and their dedication to providing the best education possible.

A New Choice

Joe Nathan, author of *Charter Schools: Creating Hope and Opportunity for American Education,* is director of the Center for School Change at the Hubert H. Humphrey Institute of Public Affairs at the University of Minnesota.

Charter schools are public schools, financed by the same public funds that traditional public schools receive. Unlike traditional public schools, however, they are held accountable for achieving educational results. In return, they receive waivers that exempt them from many of the restrictions and bureaucratic rules that shape traditional public schools. The charter school movement brings together, for the first time in public education, four powerful ideas:

- Choice among public schools for families and their children
- Entrepreneurial opportunities for educators and parents to create the kinds of schools they believe make the most sense

- Explicit responsibility for improved achievement, as measured by standardized tests and other measures
- Carefully designed competition in public education

The Differences Between Charter Schools and Other School Reforms

I like the fact that my children can play with their neighborhood friends.
Bill, father of Travis, 7, and Eric, 8

School choice is a powerful tool, something like electricity. Carefully used, choice and electricity do good things. But badly used, electricity and school choice create more problems than they solve. The details of choice programs are critical to their success.

■ **School vouchers.** Under a school voucher system, families would be given certificates (vouchers) for a set amount of money. They could then use these vouchers to pay tuition at their choice of public, private, or parochial schools. Numerous voucher proposals have been put forward. However, virtually all have been defeated, either by state legislatures or in popular referendums. The charter school differs from the voucher concept in four ways. First, charter schools must be nonsectarian. Second, in most states, the charter school legislation does not allow schools to choose among applicants on the basis of previous achievement. Third, voucher proposals usually permit private and parochial schools to charge additional tuition beyond the state allocation they receive via the voucher. A final difference between charter schools and voucher proposals concerns explicit responsibility for documenting improvement. To keep their charters, charter schools must demonstrate that their students are improving their skills and expanding their knowledge.

■ **Magnet schools.** Magnet schools are public schools with specialized curricula designed to attract particular students from throughout a school district. They are often part of an urban district's desegregation program, intended to bring together students of different races. Unlike other public schools, however, many magnet schools have admissions tests. Magnet schools spend more per student than other schools in their district. In contrast, it is a key element in the charter school strategy that charter schools receive the same as, and no more than the state per-pupil average spent on education. For charter school advocates, the issue of financial equity is critical: If charter schools are to demonstrate the value of school choice and show the worth of innovative teaching methods, they must be able to do their work and improve students' learning for the same average amount spent per public school pupil in the state.

Twenty years from now, will the charter movement be a chapter or a footnote in school reform? The charter movement's first five years have been a time of remarkable growth, fierce political struggle, and intense media interest. Yet it is impossible to know what lies ahead.

What we do know is that we will make progress as we give new opportunities to creative, committed, and talented educators who are willing to be held accountable for results. We must use this country's extraordinary entrepreneurial energy, which has produced products and services that people throughout the world want to own. Strong charter school laws will give new opportunities and encouragement to some of our talented and energetic educators. We will have fewer frustrated educators, more involved families, and more successful students.

Reading

- -

Alex learned to read in the second grade. One night before he went to sleep, as I was reading a fairly complex story to him, he said, "You missed a word."

"How do you know?" I asked in shock.

"Because I read it."

"You read it? What else can you read?"

He proceeded to read me the next paragraph. I screamed for Bernie to come into the bedroom. When he came running in because he was sure something was terribly wrong, I shrieked, "Alex knows how to read."

"He knows how to read?" he asked with amazement.

Sure enough, Alex read another paragraph to Bernie. We both laughed and wondered if we hadn't been attentive enough to Alex's school activities.

While this story about Alex's latent reading ability used to seem funny to me and my friends, it's not funny to the new crop of kindergarten moms and dads. In fact, even my friend Donna was stressed to the max when her youngest son, Benjie, wasn't reading in kindergarten.

"Why are you so concerned?" I asked.

"Because he's been in kindergarten for four months and he can't read."

"So what? When did Willa [her older daughter who was Alex's classmate] learn to read?"

"In kindergarten. That's why Sal [her husband] and I are so worried."

"For goodness' sake, Donna," I said, "when did you turn into one of 'those' mothers?" When our kids were in kindergarten together, we would joke about the pushy and competitive moms who wanted their children to be the first and the best at everything.

"It's easy for you to say. Things are different from when Alex and Willa were in kindergarten. There's way more pressure to learn how to read early."

"Do you mean to tell me his teacher is concerned about this?"

"No," she said, pausing for a moment.

"Then who is?" I asked.

She bowed her head and murmured, "Me."

"Why?" I said quizzically.

"Because five of the twenty kids in Benjie's class know how to read. Some of the parents whose kids don't know how are sending them to a special after-school reading program. Others are drilling their kids every night with flash cards. I just don't want Benjie to get too far behind."

"C'mon, Donna," I said. "For crying out loud, there were three kids in Alex and Willa's kindergarten class who knew how to read from the get-go. Not because their parents taught them, but because they just knew how. Willa was one of the first from the next group, but Alex didn't read until two years later. And when he started, he was reading at a fourth-grade level. Why are you so worried about Benjie?"

"What if he's learning disabled?" she asked.

"I don't know if they can even tell in kindergarten," I responded. "What did his teacher tell you?"

Our class has a reading center, which is a little area in class with two low bookshelves and a rocking chair. Every afternoon the teacher reads to the children. My daughter can actually sound out words; it's amazing.

Karen, mother of
Rami, 6

"Not to worry."

"Then stop worrying. Aren't you aware of why there's this sudden pressure to teach kids how to read, write, and do math?"

"I know it's about the testing, but that doesn't make me feel better."

"In other words, even though you know that school district policy makers are putting pressure on the teachers and principals to bring up the reading test scores, and that some children are just not developmentally ready to read, you're still concerned?"

"Well," she said, pausing, and I finally relaxed because I was sure she was regaining her sanity, "what about phonics?"

"What about it?"

"Do you think Benjie should be tutored in phonics?"

"No, I don't. I think the real issue is that everything is getting out of hand. I assume that there is a time when a child's inability to read becomes a problem, and I would assume that his teachers will recognize it. If they don't, then you might ask for a special evaluation."

"How will I know when to ask?"

"Donna," I now said with total frustration. "I know we haven't seen each other for a while but yikes, when did you get so neurotic?"

She finally laughed. "Now that you put it that way, it does seem ridiculous, doesn't it?"

I rolled my eyeballs. "I think you've been hanging around with the wrong group. Kindergarten parents are too stressed; just think of how we used to be. But now that our kids are in fifth grade, nothing phases us."

"So where are you going to send Alex to middle school?" she asked with a twinkle in her eye.

"All right!" I admitted. "So there are a few concerns remaining."

"Gotcha!" she said.

All I could do was shake my head.

Reading and Language Arts

Michael F. Graves is a professor of curriculum and instruction at The University of Minnesota–Twin Cities and coauthor of *Teaching Reading in the 21st Century* and *The Essentials of Elementary Reading*.

What are the components of an excellent kindergarten reading program?

There are three components to a good kindergarten reading program. What's important to remember is that they can't be prioritized; all must be included. The first component is to help kids become comfortable with school in the formal classroom setting. The second component is to give kids basic knowledge about the form and function of print. The third component is to instill in children a desire to read, a budding love and appreciation of reading, an interest in books and other reading materials, and confidence that they can learn to read. So the three of them are getting used to school, learning some relatively formal things about print and reading, and affective concerns about liking reading and feeling that it is something they want and can learn to do. People tend to gravitate toward one end or the other, but it is essential to include all three components in a balanced way.

The second component needs some explanation. Knowledge about the basic form and function of print includes learning that

- print, like talk, conveys meaning; that a child's own speech can be recorded in print and read by him- or herself and others
- books and other reading materials contain stories and other sorts of things
- you read from left to right, top to bottom, and front to back
- books have words

- words are the things separated by spaces and are composed of individual letters
- letters represent sounds

Our school has a reading class for parents who have just come to this country. Those of us who speak English teach others. Children teach their parents.

Kuri, mother of Elizabeth, 7, and Min Ting, 10

The second component also includes the development of phonemic awareness, or the knowledge that words are composed of somewhat separable sounds. Phonemic awareness is important because if kids cannot hear and appreciate that words are made up of somewhat separable sounds, then trying to instruct them in phonics (the relationship between the sounds and the letters) is just nonsense to them. Educators only recently recognized the importance of phonemic awareness. The problem now is that having figured out the importance of phonemic awareness, some schools and even states have decided they will promote it with a vengeance, more of a vengeance than it deserves. The message here is that a lot of things are important, not just one component. For example, in addition to gaining phonemic awareness, kids ought to leave kindergarten recognizing and probably being able to print most of the letters of the alphabet.

Which teaching method is best, or is that an issue?

We do not talk as much about method in kindergarten as we would in first grade and beyond, certainly. If method is interpreted as what the teacher values or spends her or his time doing, then the method should ensure that all three components receive appropriate amounts of time. If you have teachers concerned only with the affective components of reading, the nearly solitary goal is to get kids to love books, and that is not going to work. On the other hand, if you have teachers whose primary goal is to get them to learn some of the mechanics of reading, then that is wrong too. All three of the components I've listed are essential. A teacher with a bent toward the phonic method or one with a bent toward the whole language approach needs to be sure that all three components receive attention if the reading program is going to work well.

What questions should parents of kindergartners ask when evaluating a school's reading program?

- Does the school attend to all three of those components, and to what extent? What you are looking for is balance.

- How is what the school does in kindergarten articulated, connected, and coordinated with what is done in first grade and beyond?

- To what extent has the kindergarten program been constructed in view of the fact that kids may be moving to another school or district?

Mrs. Alphabet

Anne Lynch, better known as Mrs. Alphabet, has been a kindergarten teacher for thirty-two years and now develops materials for teaching the alphabet. She lives in Parklands, Florida.

Learning the ABCs may be easy for some children, but others struggle and need a more fundamental approach. Like crawling before walking, the alphabet is the structural model for learning phonetic awareness, sight words, and reading. Mrs. Alphabet is my name, and teaching the alphabet is my game.

Alphabet recognition can set the tone for the child's future success as an accomplished learner. I have found that the most favorable methods of teaching the alphabet depend on the learning style of the child.

■ Associational cues jog the memory and help the child sift through prior knowledge to recall the name of the letter. My Alphabet Kids contain the letter at the beginning of the character's name. For example, *E* for Eve, *G* for Gina, and *P* for Peter. Then you can ask which one of Mrs. Alphabet's kids likes to paint. The answer is Peter, of course.

The children keep a journal and write in it twice a day. They write words as they hear them without any correction. The teacher has all the children sign in every day so that both we and they can see their progress.

Catherine, mother of Claudia, 2, and Nina, 6

■ Some children are auditory learners and pick up on what they hear to learn the alphabet. Alphabet songs, fingerplays, and poems can assist some students in mastering the alphabet.

■ Visual models of the letters can come to life if you tell a story or follow a sequence to help children learn. I have little stories and poems for each letter of the alphabet. For example, *C* is a cookie that has a bite taken out of it, *M* is a mountain, and *S* is a snake. Pointing to the letters and singing the alphabet also reinforces a strong visual model. Color codes, fanciful sets of letters, alphabet books, and flash cards continue to increase identification and recall of the alphabet.

■ Kinesthetic activities that involve the children in the learning process strengthen the skills of discovering the names of the letters. Games, puzzles, computer software, interactive games on the Internet, and movements that stress distinguishing the alphabet through hands-on lessons increase the recognition procedure.

Remember children differ in how they process information, and the more strategies, print-rich environment, and balanced curriculum you provide the better the chances of children mastering the alphabet. Once the child knows the alphabet, he or she can continue to develop more advanced skills such as phonics, rhyming, sequencing, alphabetical order, printing, chunking, and reading.

Report Cards

"When Joey was in kindergarten, the report cards were indecipherable," said Nat, a single working father. "There were seven classifications. Communications skills had three subheads: oral language, written language, and reading. The other categories were mathematics, social studies, science, fine arts, physical education, and work habits and social development.

"Under every heading and subheading were bullets denoting the specific variables for which Joey would be evaluated. For example, in math he would be graded on whether he understood math concepts and applied them. In oral language, did he continue to increase his speaking vocabulary and did he use grammatical forms in thinking? Could he use critical thinking skills in reading? And could he apply learned information to new situations in social studies?

"And what about his work habits and social development? Personally, I had no idea how his teacher would evaluate whether he tried to do his best and observed standards. It was probably much easier to evaluate whether he listened attentively, followed directions, and worked well with others.

I don't understand the purpose of report cards in kindergarten. The parent conferences and portfolios have a far better value.

Nathan, father of Mathew, 7, and Jeffrey, 10

179

What totally baffles me is that the report card wasn't reflective of the information I received in the parent conference. I can't imagine why. Perhaps the teacher felt she could be more honest when we talked together and didn't want to hurt my child's feelings by giving her a bad report card.

Cybil, mother of
Bruce, 5, and
Sabrina, 7

"I must admit that my performance appraisals at work aren't that rigorous. All told there were 37 categories.

"Doing some quick addition, I figured that if his teacher evaluated 32 children in 37 categories, she had to determine 1,184 grades midsemester and the same at the end of the year. I couldn't imagine how she could possibly assess each child when she was working from a pool of 2,368 grades.

"What made this even more confusing was that the children were not graded on a scale of A to F, as we had been when we were kids. In Joey's kindergarten, the classifications were 'almost always,' 'sometimes,' and 'not yet.'

"Still, when he came home from school and together we looked at his report card he proudly said, 'Dad, I got 35 A's and 2 B's. David [a third-grade friend] told me.'

"'That's very good,' I replied.

"'Know why I got the B's?' he asked.

"'Nope.'

"'Because during music, I move my lips but I don't sing, and I hit Daytwon.'

"'Why do you hit Daytwon?' I asked with surprise, since Daytwon is his best friend.

"'He doesn't listen to my words. The teacher said to use our words, but when he doesn't listen, I hit him.'

"Even though I knew we would later have to have one of those father-son discussions on how we handle our impatience or frustrations in a more socially acceptable manner, I tried not to smile. I actually thought his solution might be helpful for me at work. First you talk, then you hit.

"'Daytwon got a B because he hits me when I don't listen.'

"'Oh,' I casually said. It seemed fair to me; a little quid pro quo sounded like a good resolution.

"Later, after Joey had gone to sleep, I looked at his report card once again. I liked the teacher's comments best. He wrote, 'Joey is an enthusiastic learner and his thoughtfulness and insights add much to our class discussions.'

"This time I could smile without restraint."

Determining Kindergartners' Abilities

Stuart Reifel, Ed.D., is professor of curriculum and instruction at the University of Texas at Austin, where he teaches in the early childhood education program.

What is the importance of assessment in kindergarten?

Assessment is important because it tells us whether children are progressing and if they are having difficulties with certain aspects of their development. If a child has difficulty making friends or attending to the story at story time, it may suggest that further observation and assessment be done; the child may need special help relating to others, or may have a hearing problem. Assessment should provide insight into the particular needs and strengths of a child, and there should always be multiple forms of assessment. A decision about a child should never be based on one assessment.

What is the purpose of report cards?

There are so many different types of report cards. Some give letter grades for performance on academic tasks, even in kindergarten. Others describe a child's relative performance of normative skills, for example, identifying letters, naming colors, or following directions. Other reports may be narrative, describing a child's strengths, weaknesses, and progress. I believe that the report card itself may not tell parents much. The report card should serve as a basis for much more extensive discussions with the teacher about the child's educational engagement.

Why are kindergarten report cards so confusing?

Professionals and nonprofessionals have different ideas about what purpose a report card should have and what should be included on one. A complex report card may reflect professionals' opinions about what should be reported, but it may be reported in a manner that needs translation to nonprofessionals. Children are complex (aren't we all?) and deserve a thoughtful assessment. The report card may not be the best method to communicate a thoughtful assessment.

What is the best method of assessment?

Either they should give the kids letter grades or not grade them at all.
Zack, father of Nick, 8

Kindergarten children vary a great deal in their developmental levels and abilities. The best way to assess each child is in terms of his or her own progress on a number of developmental and learning dimensions. Think about the following questions: What progress is this child making in terms of social development? What progress is this child making in terms of symbol use and expression? What progress is this child making in terms of play relationships? What progress is this child making in terms of identifying and pursuing interests, such as reading storybooks, writing stories, drawing, building, or playing games?

What is portfolio assessment?

There are many different forms of portfolio assessments, but they all demonstrate a belief that the best reflection of a child's performance is a set of materials that the child has created in the classroom. Portfolios may include stories that the child has written, pictures that have been drawn, the child's report of a science project, or other products of activities that the child has experienced.

Are there other types of assessment?

There are many forms of assessment. We may be most familiar with tests, whether written, performance, standardized, or criterion referenced. Given the ways that young children develop, tests tend not to be a good gauge of how they can perform. Other forms of assessment, including observations of children in the classroom while they are engaged in learning activities, tend to tell teachers more about children.

Reporting Progress

Doug Shrivers is a kindergarten teacher at Hall Elementary School in Gresham, Oregon.

If a report card is designed correctly, the different categories presented allow the parents to participate effectively in their child's education. For instance, the report card I use has two categories that deal with letters: recognizes letters and associates letters with sounds. Although these two categories give a general idea of whether the child is learning the names of letters and the letter sounds, parents cannot tell how many letters or letter sounds the child knows and which ones they should be helping the child with at home. To correct this, I attach a separate sheet to the report card that specifies with checked boxes the specific letters and letter sounds that the child knows.

In addition, I added a category to specify whether the child uses these letters to try to compose words. With this knowledge the parent can make up little games that will help the child work on the concepts. For example, if the *b* sound was not checked, the child can go on a treasure hunt around the house to find objects that start with that sound. Another category on the original report card is "identifies basic colors." What exactly does this mean? If the box is checked, parents would know that their child can identify whatever is considered a basic color. However, if the box is unchecked, a child could be having trouble with one color (such as gray) or all the colors. To clarify things, I added a check box for all the eleven colors that I consider basic. That way the parent knows what color the child needs to work on. And, as with letters, parents can engage their children in fun games to reinforce the color names. If orange is the problem color, you and your child could draw an all-orange picture. You could also go through magazines and cut out pictures of anything that was orange and paste it into a collage. As you can see, if a

What's so funny is that the students aren't supposed to show each other their report cards, but they do—even in kindergarten.

Miles, father of Charlotte, 8, and Brian, 10

report card is done correctly, the parent becomes a partner with the teacher in helping the child learn.

One thing to be careful of, however, is the attempt by some schools to push academic subjects onto kindergartners, a product of the current drive to add standardized testing to virtually every grade level. Before you enroll your child in kindergarten, ask to see the report card used. If it is full of what seems like an overabundance of categories such as "colors within the lines," "completes worksheets on time," "reads books without error," and "spells words correctly," you should try to observe the class (this would be a good thing to do in any case). Kindergarten should be a fun place where children learn by experimenting with new ideas and interacting with their fellow students. It should not be a place where children spend too much time working at their desks, completing activity sheets, and doing homework assignments. For many children, kindergarten is their first school experience, and it should be a positive and joyful introduction to the world of education.

Science

---

hen Alex received his first kindergarten grade in science, I asked Bernie if he knew that Alex was learning science.

"Honey, of course," Bernie patiently replied, knowing that math and science aren't my strong suits.

"What do you mean 'of course'?" I asked. "I don't see him working with chemical elements over a Bunsen burner, dissecting a frog, or memorizing body parts."

"Susan, he's only in kindergarten," Bernie said, with exasperation.

"I'm just kidding," I replied. "I know we don't let him play with fire. He's not allowed to use a knife. I guess he'd have to learn how to read before he could memorize the names of bones and muscles. But seriously, what does a kindergarten science curriculum encompass?"

Without a pause, he said, "Weather."

"What about it? The teacher asks the kids what kind of day it is. They say 'good' or 'very good.' After all, this is Los Angeles," I said.

"You do know that people in other states actually have seasons?" he said with some hesitation.

"Of course. I was kidding."

I'm glad they are teaching science in kindergarten. With all the computer and video games in this world, I think it's important for children to go outdoors.

Naomi, mother of
Jacob, 5, and
Nora, 8

"What about plants?" he asked.

"What about them?" I responded. "Alex put an avocado seed with toothpicks sticking out into a bottle of water and it's growing roots. By the time it's a full-fledged tree, we'll all be dead. So what's the point?"

Bernie laughed, paused for a moment, then seriously asked, "Do I really need to point out that when Alex and the rest of his class learn how to identify roots, stems, leaves, and flowers, it's called 'science'? The realization that our bodies need water, fruits, vegetables, nuts, legumes, and other organic elements the earth provides is also science."

"I think you're overestimating the kids' understanding of these concepts," I responded. "Let's ask Alex and Roger. They're in the same class."

We called the boys into the family room. "I've got a few questions for you guys," I said. "Think of it as a guessing game."

"Okay," they replied with enthusiasm.

"Where do apples come from?"

"Oh Mom," Alex said, with embarrassment. "Apple trees."

"Good answer," I said. "What about corn?"

"Cornstalks," Roger yelled with glee. "My grandpa has a farm. They grow corn."

I looked over at Bernie, who was smugly smiling as if he'd made his point.

"Last question, boys," I said, with a final card up my sleeve. "What about french fries?"

Bernie glared at me as if I were taking unfair advantage.

The boys looked at each other. Roger whispered something to Alex. He nodded and they both yelled, "McDonald's!"

I did a thumbs-up, smiling at Bernie to confirm I'd made my point. He shook his head to suggest I wasn't playing by the rules. I turned to the boys and asked, "How about a Happy Meal?"

They clapped their hands and cheered as we drove to McDonald's. When we arrived and they told me what they

My daughter loves science. She particularly likes it when they teach the unit about animal babies. I'm not so sure. She has begun begging my husband and me to give her a sibling.

Darla, mother of Paula, 7

wanted, I waited at the cashier, and they stood off to the side, whispering together.

Once we sat down to eat, Alex and Roger looked at each other and took a collective gulp. "What's wrong, guys? Don't you like your food?" I asked, munching on my quarter pounder with cheese.

"Uh-huh," they quietly said in unison.

"Then what's the problem?" I asked, sipping my malt.

"Potatoes," Alex whispered.

"Potatoes?" I asked in confusion.

"Grandpa told me french fries come from potatoes," Roger glumly said. "I told Alex."

"But we decided to say McDonald's anyway," Alex admitted.

"Why?"

"We wanted the toys."

I laughed inside, not wanting to encourage lying. Who wouldn't tell a white lie for a Happy Meal? My lecture on honesty would have to come later. I didn't want my french fries to get cold.

A World of Exploration

Judith P. Kesselman, M.A., a senior conservation educator and staff developer at the Tiorati Workshop for Environmental Learning, teaches early childhood, elementary, and middle school teachers how to integrate science into their curriculum.

What is your philosophy for teaching kindergarten science?

Early childhood science should be part of what is already in a child's world. Children begin exploring the world from the time they are born. They explore with their mouths. As they get older, they explore in a variety of ways, using their hands, eyes, noses, ears, and with supervision, touching and manipulating. We need to facilitate this curiosity and not get in the way.

Our younger son kept asking us if they would be teaching science in kindergarten. He wouldn't say why. But on the very first day of kindergarten, he asked his teacher if he would be able to make flubber like the nutty professor [in the film].

Harvey, father of
Dex, 8, and
Keith, 11

When we teach science in kindergarten, we need to zero in on what they are already familiar with. For example, we all eat apples. We all know that the apple has a stem and there are seeds inside and so on. We eat it and we throw it away. We don't look at it. In kindergarten science, we ask the children to look closely at the apple, smell it, describe it, and compare the different colors. Each child in the class has an apple to explore. What makes an apple an apple? What makes all apples different? The teacher then cuts one in half so the kids can see the connections, such as how the stem attaches to the core. The teacher talks about what the stem is and how it holds the apple on the tree from which it gets the nutrients that help the apple develop. And there is this fuzzy little thing on the bottom of the apple, which also connects to the core. It's the remains of the flower. Then the teachers can get out some books that show pictures of apples in various stages of development. The key is to explore something that the children know about. In early childhood, if we can focus on helping children look closely and see things that they otherwise would skip, then we're teaching them science.

Kids are natural scientists. They're busy exploring, classifying, and discovering patterns as part of their everyday life. If your five- or six-year-old child helps you set the table, the child is learning a pattern. There are patterns in everything. There's a pattern in getting up in the morning, getting dressed, brushing the teeth, eating breakfast, and going off to school. Those patterns translate into science, such as the seasons or the phases of the moon. We can help children begin to develop that kind of awareness with familiar things in their environment.

We can go further by bringing animals, such as mealworms, earthworms, and snails, into the classroom or into the home so that the children can help care for them. The kids are now exposed to a living thing that is a little more foreign than an apple, and they can develop an awareness of what the creature is like, what its needs are, and what changes it goes through. It is important that the kinds of activities we do are things that are in the immediate environment, in the class-room, in the kitchen, in the bathroom, in the yard, and in the trees outside. If you show them something glitzy, you might get their attention, but they may not learn from it.

How can science be integrated into the curriculum?

While kids are learning science, they are also expanding their vocabulary and learning to compare and contrast. Developing vocabulary with descriptive words is the basis of science, and it feeds right into social studies and language arts. Spatial relation concepts are part of science, and they feed right into math. When you teach science, you are getting into all of these subjects. I don't think you can teach kindergarten children science as an isolated subject because it is bound to spill over into math, language arts, and social studies.

When children study the seasons, they are learning about science and also about how we dress in the winter and what we do in our homes in the winter, and all of that ties together beautifully. A typical unit in kindergarten is the family. When you talk about family, you are classifying. Who are the people in the family? What are their roles? That's social studies, but it's also science—a discipline that provides a world of exploration.

I'm a lab technician. I only wish I had been able to begin studying science in kindergarten like my children. Perhaps I could have been a doctor.

Su-Ling, mother of Erin, 7

Social Studies

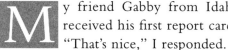

If social studies teaches children to learn to live together, then it may be the most important subject that's taught.

Tom, father of
Harry, 8, and
Fay, 10

My friend Gabby from Idaho called. "Lukas just received his first report card."

"That's nice," I responded.

"He got a 'sometimes' in a subject with the following criteria: 'Can identify and solve problems. Uses various ways of obtaining information. Applies learned information to new situations.' "

"What's the subject?" I asked.

"It doesn't ring a bell?"

"Sounds rather vague. How am I supposed to know?"

"Because for the last six years, Alex has received grades in this subject."

"Beats me!" I exclaimed.

"Social studies."

"Sounds reasonable."

"What do you think kindergarten social studies encompasses?"

"Listen, I had a difficult enough time defining science," I responded.

"What did Alex learn in social studies?"

"I have no idea. What is Lukas learning?" I asked.

"How can I tell if I don't know what social studies means?"

"Why don't you ask his teacher?"

"Because I don't want to sound like a moron. What will he think of me when I tell him I took social studies from elementary through secondary school and I have no idea what it means?"

"That you're intellectually challenged?" I asked. She didn't even chuckle.

"Ask your mother. After all, you had four siblings. Maybe she remembers."

"I did; she doesn't."

"Look it up in the dictionary."

"I did. *Webster's New World College Dictionary* says, and I quote, 'a course of study especially in elementary and secondary school, including history, civics, and geography.'"

"So what's your question?"

"Why did Lukas get a 'sometimes' as a grade? Does that mean sometimes he knows we live in Idaho and sometimes he thinks we live in Georgia? Sometimes he thinks we're governed by a president and sometime he thinks it's a queen? Sometimes he knows that we're citizens of the United States and sometimes he thinks we're citizens of Bali?"

"I hear Bali is a great place to visit."

When Gabby didn't laugh, I quietly asked, "Do you think you might be overreacting?"

She paused. "Do you think so?"

"If Lukas had gotten an 'always' in social studies, would you have cared about any of this?"

"Of course not," she said, and finally laughed.

Learning About Each Other

This is an abridged version of "Social Studies for Early Childhood and Elementary School Children: Preparing for the 21st Century," a position statement of the National Council for Social Studies.

Because our student population has a large number of immigrants, social studies is critical. Kindergarten is a good place to start the entire process.

Toby, mother of Ernie, 7, and Leon, 9

What are the goals for elementary school social studies?

The elementary school years are important in that they are the ones in which children develop a foundation for the entire social studies program. Knowledge, skills, and attitudes necessary for informed and thoughtful participation in society require a systematically developed program focusing on concepts from history and the social sciences.

■ **Knowledge.** Social studies provide a sense of history, a sense of existence in the past as well as the present, a feeling of being in history. Even though young children find the concept of time difficult, they need to understand how the present has come about and to develop an appreciation for the heritage of this country.

■ **Skills.** The skills that are primary to social studies are those related to maps and globes, such as understanding and using locational and directional terms. Skills that are shared with other parts of the curriculum but may be most powerfully taught through social studies include

- communication skills such as writing and speaking
- research skills such as collecting, organizing, and interpreting data
- thinking skills such as hypothesizing, comparing, drawing inferences
- decision-making skills such as considering alternatives and consequences
- interpersonal skills such as seeing others' points of view, accepting responsibility, and dealing with conflict
- reading skills such as reading pictures, books, maps, charts, and graphs

■ **Attitudes.** The early years are ideal for children to begin to understand democratic norms and values, especially in terms of the smaller social entities of the family, classroom, and community.

Although not uniquely in social studies, children can achieve a positive self-concept within the context of understanding the similarities and differences of people. Children need to understand that they are unique in themselves but share many similar feelings and concerns with other children. They need to understand how as individuals they can contribute to society.

What criteria should be considered in planning a social studies program?

First, we need to consider that children of all ages come to school from different socioeconomic and cultural backgrounds. They come with different values, experiences, and learning styles, and with different feelings about themselves and the people around them.

Most five-year-olds can begin to combine simple ideas into more complex relationships. They have a growing memory capacity and fine motor physical skills. They have a growing interest in the functional aspects of written language, such as recognizing meaningful words and trying to write their names. They need an environment rich in printed materials that stimulates the development of language and literacy skills in a meaningful context. They also need a variety of direct experiences to develop cognitively, physically, emotionally, and socially. Since five-year-olds come to school with an interest in the community and the world outside their own home, curriculum can expand beyond the child's immediate experience of self, home, and family.

Six-year-olds are active learners and demonstrate considerable verbal ability. They are interested in games and rules and develop concepts and problem-solving skills from these experiences. Hands-on activity and experimentation are necessary for this age group.

Kindergartners become more aware of social perspective. The focus on relationships between people and their environments in elementary social studies is derived from the assumption that young children need to understand both their own

As far as I'm concerned, if the only thing kindergartners learned about social studies was the importance of voting, our democratic system would have a better chance.

Patty, mother of Chuck, 7, and Nalsey, 9

uniqueness and their relationship to the world. Social judgments also involve more than the child's "getting along" in the home or school environment. Research on how children acquire these understandings indicates that children are more open to diversity in the early elementary years than in later years.

Positive self-concepts, important in positively perceiving and judging social interactions, also form during these crucial early years. Particular classroom environments seem to influence the ways children develop these interactions. Teachers who appear to enjoy teaching, who include great student-to-student interaction, shared decision making, and positive student-to-teacher interactions foster more positive self-concepts in their pupils.

What can we learn from social studies?

Society is characterized by increasingly rapid social and technological change. Our culture's ability to orchestrate change frequently outstrips its ability to reflect on the ramifications of what it has done. Are our children developing the necessary skills to absorb new information in light of this information explosion?

When they leave the classroom, many children do not return immediately to the family setting but go to a day-care facility where they again interact with others from a variety of backgrounds. Nearly all children spend more hours each week watching television than they spend in any other activity besides sleeping. As they sit passively watching, they are bombarded by messages. They take in spotty, disconnected information about war, the homeless, crime, and politics. Are they learning any structures for interpreting this information and fitting it into a larger framework? Commercial television networks see children as an economic force and press them to make consumer decisions. Are children learning to evaluate these messages, or do they continue to sit passively as they are manipulated? These are the questions we need to address.

Consider a kindergarten class in any one of thousands of school systems in the United States. How do the children

As everyone becomes more concerned about math and science, even in kindergarten, they are forgetting that social studies helps our children learn about the entire world. When my son saw his first globe, he was mesmerized.

Frank, father of Frank Jr., 6, and Devon, 9

in the class experience the world? Their classroom mirrors the larger society with its diverse ethnic, religious, and socioeconomic backgrounds. Are the children learning structures for accepting and appreciating diversity at this critical age in the development of lifelong attitudes? Mere contact with diversity, without understanding, can intensify conflict. Does their classroom mirror the larger society in this sense also? Kindergarten teachers and parents need to be aware of these issues.

Special Needs Children

One afternoon, Ginny, the mother of three children—her oldest two, a daughter and son, are special needs children—came over to talk about her experiences. After the usual chitchat, she asked, "What do you want to know?"

"What was it like for your kids in kindergarten?" I asked somewhat hesitantly. Even though she had agreed to be interviewed, I was feeling slightly uncomfortable about how to ask the questions I was interested in.

Ginny quickly put me at ease. "It's not an easy answer," she said, "because you really need some history leading up to kindergarten."

I nodded. She continued.

"We weren't sure Brooke was developmentally challenged, as they call it," she said shaking her head as if to indicate that she didn't care what the politically correct terminology was, "until she was in preschool."

"As an infant and toddler, she seemed fine. She was our first child, so we had no means of comparison, and her pediatrician never suggested anything was wrong. By the time she was in preschool, she was clearly lagging behind. Still, both the preschool director and the pediatrician gave me the standard lecture about the variances between children's growth, learning abilities, and so on.

"In the meantime, Arlen was born and within a year diagnosed as autistic."

I didn't know what to say but wondered how she managed to remain so positive.

"I've got to tell you," she said, "that was the most devastating day of my life. By this time we still had no idea what was wrong with Brooke. She had had a multitude of tests, and then this. I was so grateful my mother was with me when the neurologist gave me the news, because I felt like my heart had been ripped from my body. Once we came home, I went into my bedroom and cried for the next thirty-six hours."

"How did Neal [her husband] handle it?" I gently asked.

Ginny smiled. "He was quiet for a few days. The third day he walked into the bedroom, looked me straight in the eyes and said, 'Ginny, I guess Arlen won't be a lawyer. Thank God for that.'

"We both laughed until we cried," Ginny said, "and that was when I stopped feeling sorry for myself and determined that I would be more aggressive in finding help for both my children. You see, there are so many issues with special needs kids. If you can believe it, finding help for Brooke was actually more difficult than finding help for Arlen."

I looked at her quizzically. She shook her head, fully understanding my confusion.

"You see, Brooke has problems, but they are not easily identifiable. First they thought she was borderline autistic. Then they decided she wasn't but that she had learning disabilities. Her speech has always lagged behind kids her own age, and she was never as socially mature.

"The lack of a diagnosis made it extremely difficult to determine what her school needs were. Ultimately, we enrolled her in a public school with a strong special education program. She has always been mainstreamed and has been provided with an aide. It has worked out fairly well. In cer-

*W*hether your children should be mainstreamed or not is a real decision. On one hand, you want them to have a "normal" experience. On the other hand, they might not get the help they need.

> Dorothy, mother of Barbie, 7, Elaine, 9, and Kathy, 16

tain ways, she hasn't progressed as much as we would have liked. But it's difficult to know what she's capable of learning since we still don't have an accurate diagnosis.

"Although Arlen's disability is 'worse,' it has been easier to find help for him. Autism is a defined disability, and there is a recommended plan of action. By the age of two-and-a-half, we sent him to a special school. Early intervention is critical, and that's part of the program. He has been eligible for private speech therapy, physical therapy, sensory stimulation, and a number of other services.

"When it was time for him to attend kindergarten, we enrolled him in the same school we had found for Brooke. He learned to talk in the second grade and has made huge progress. We don't know what he will be able to accomplish as he progresses, but we take it one day at a time."

"So entering kindergarten was all right?" I asked.

She closed her eyes for a moment, remembering back almost five years earlier when Brooke started kindergarten. "With Brooke, I was almost as concerned about social acceptance as I was about her educational needs being met. Because she's shy and 'different,' we weren't sure how she would be accepted by the other children or their parents. But everything worked out fine.

"A few weeks after school started, a little girl named Eleanor invited her over for a play date. Brooke was excited. I was a nervous wreck. When we arrived at Eleanor's house, I was immediately relieved. There was a kind of warmth, it is difficult to describe, and the house was full of kids. Mary and her husband, Earl, who both came from large families themselves, have eight children.

"Anyway, the moment we arrived, Eleanor took Brooke's hand, and while they ran off to play, I had a long talk with Eleanor's mother, Mary. We really hit it off. Within moments, I, who rarely talk about my children's problems, was pouring my heart out. Mary was an unbelievable listener. She said that when people come from large families, they are used to being around kids who have disabilities. One of her sisters has a terrible stuttering problem, and Earl's youngest sister contracted a rare disease when she was twelve, almost died, and although she survived, lost her sight. Even I was speechless," Ginny admitted.

"The great thing is that five years later, although Brooke has made only a few other friends, she and Eleanor are still best friends. The Logan family has become our extended family. Arlen has become friends with David, who at five is the baby in their family. Almost every day, I thank my lucky stars that Eleanor took Brooke under her wing.

"When Neal and I look back on the last eleven years, we have to smile. While we never thought our lives with our children would turn out like this, we feel blessed. As Neal always says, 'We couldn't love children any more than we love ours. We must have been specially picked to be Brooke and Arlen's parents.'

"'What about Jay?' I ask Neal. He is the youngest and has no disabilities.

"'Him too,' Neal says with a twinkle in his eyes."

Determining Who Has Special Needs

Michael S. Rosenberg, Ph.D., is a professor and chair of the Department of Special Education at Johns-Hopkins University.

What services do most public schools offer kindergarten children with special needs?

The services offered vary from state to state and from locality to locality. Different schools organize their services for kids with special needs in different ways. Children with more severe needs have usually been identified before entering kindergarten, and because of their history, immediately are offered special services. For example, a child with language development problems might be teamed up with a language specialist who will take that child out of the classroom each day for a specified period of time and work with him or her on specific skills. Some districts may have behavioral specialists on staff to work with children who clearly have problems in this area. On the whole, the services offered depend on the severity of the disability and whether the disability has been identified.

My son's kindergarten teacher was a saint. With her volunteers and her aide, she truly helped the children who needed it, without having them feel different.

Carla, mother of
Oliver, 6, and
Alana, 9

In kindergarten, because there is a vast range of behavior and skill among children this age, a disability may not be identified unless it is severe. For many children, some of whom have not been in preschool, there may be dramatic differences in language usage, quality of speech, behavioral functioning, and socialization. So in kindergarten, teachers try to assess the children by looking at different developmental profiles. Some kids conform; others do not. The differences in language and behavioral functioning are often signs of possible disabilities. The children whose needs are identified will receive special services. What happens to those who are not identified depends upon the school district and the state.

Kindergarten teachers are trained to look for disabilities, but it's a gray area. On one hand, one cannot underestimate the value of early identification and intervention. On the other hand, mistaken identification and intervention can be a problem as well. If children's learning or behavioral problems are developmental in nature and eventually will work themselves out through sound instruction in a stimulating environment, it would be a disservice—with all the attendant stigmatization—to separate those children from the general population. Ideally, school districts are hiring good people who not only understand the development of children and the wide range of abilities and behaviors, but also understand those thresholds where certain behaviors tip off the need for early intervention.

What are the pros and cons of inclusion programs versus pull-out programs?

Based upon children's needs, a full continuum of services should be available. In an inclusion setting, a child gets all the benefits of increased socialization, provided the teacher is supported by a special educator who can offer tips on how to adapt instruction for the needs of that student. In inclusion programs, children are neither separated from their friends nor do they face the stigmatization that is sometimes prevalent when children are placed in pull-out programs. The value of a pull-out program, where children are taken out of the classroom, is that they receive more intense instruction. They are put into smaller groups, usually with one teacher. In determining a child's needs it is important to consider the goals you need to achieve. Sometimes a mixture of the two types of programs is most effective.

Where can parents get help?

First-time parents or parents who did not come from large families, in which there could have been a wide range of behavior, often do not know what to expect in terms of identification of special needs. If parents have any concerns, the first person to see is a developmental pediatrician. This is a physician who is not only expert in physical development and medical interventions, but also a specialist regarding social, cognitive, and emotional milestones in young children.

In addition, each state has a Parent Information Training Resource Center that is run by parents to support families through the maze of available services, as well as advocating for parents to help them get the right services for their kids. Parents should never be shy about asking questions or seeking help if they suspect that their child needs assistance. Early identification of a child's special needs will lead to interventions that can lead to improved educational and social/emotional development.

Teaching Special Needs Children

Colleen Gallagher is the K–3 special education teacher at Silver Ridge Elementary School in Silverdale, Washington.

My daughter's kindergarten experience was a disaster. Anything that could go wrong did. She felt stigmatized and so did we. After that year, we put her into a private school. She is much happier.

Paul, father of
Christy, 7

My philosophy of education is to make lifelong learners out of my students. I want my students to walk into the classroom with smiles on their faces and enthusiasm in their voices. We can accomplish this goal through a positive approach to learning and teaching.

In fact, through positive learning experiences, it is possible for every child to learn the desired skills. Understanding and retention are not fostered through the excessive use of workbooks and worksheets, but will flourish in an atmosphere where learning is fun. By writing and conducting stimulating lessons, teachers can make learning exciting. Relating subject matter to real-life situations will focus students' attention on the task and inspire a quest for additional knowledge. Integrated lessons reinforce prior learning and increase students' interest and understanding.

Each student learns in his or her unique way. Because all children deserve an equal chance to learn, the teacher is responsible for accommodating these unique learning styles by presenting material in a variety of ways and allowing the students to discover through hands-on experiences. Children learn more from performing activities themselves and will retain material better if they experience it rather than simply memorizing it.

With time and patience, effective learning is possible for all children. Teachers should have high expectations for every student in their class and should never underestimate what a student can achieve. If teachers encourage discovery and make material meaningful, learning will flourish in the classroom.

Parental involvement is important in shaping a child's attitude toward learning. Newsletters, classroom Internet sites, periodic telephone calls, school programs, and conferences keep parents abreast of the progress of their child and encourage an active interest in that progress.

Education is more than just teaching; it is loving, caring, communicating, and growing. By integrating all these qualities into the educational environment, the teacher will instill a love of learning in her or his students.

Teachers

-- -- -- -- -- -- -- -- -- -- -- -- -- -- -- --

One morning at drop-off time, a few weeks after school had begun, I approached a few kindergarten moms who were talking with each other. After introducing myself and explaining the nature of this book, I asked them what qualities they were looking for in their children's teachers.

The answers came fast and furious. "Warmth, patience, and experience," one mom said.

"Youth, exuberance, and enthusiasm," replied another.

"A firm grounding in developmentally appropriate behavior, realistic expectations for a five-year-old's intellectual capacity, and the ability to implement a structured classroom environment," said a woman named Constance.

Holly, a cherubic mother of seven with two children in a stroller, laughed aloud. "Gals, you sure have high standards," she said, looking around the group. "The truth is that it doesn't much matter what you want. You get who you get. Oops," she said, looking at her watch, "Seamus was due at preschool ten minutes ago. See ya!"

Holly's answer cast a pall over the group. There was a pause before Mylan, a diminutive woman who hadn't yet spoken, began. "Don't worry," she quietly said. "Holly's got a

My two children's kindergarten teacher was wonderful. She loves teaching and the children know it.

Butch, father of Kris, 7, and Nichole, 9

heart of gold, but with five children already in elementary and middle school, she has developed a rather pragmatic approach to life."

"You can say that again!" said a mom named Fari. Everyone laughed.

"My own experience," Mylan continued, "is that all the teachers at this school bring something special to the children in their classrooms. While they may have different personalities, backgrounds, teaching styles, levels of experience, interests, and hobbies, good teaching has no boundaries."

"Mylan, what do you mean by that?" asked a woman who identified herself as Cynthia.

"Think of the teachers you liked best when you were in school. What were the qualities you most admired?"

There was a moment of silence before a number of people began responding.

"Imagination."

"Love of learning."

"Compassion."

"Silliness quotient," answered a woman named Julia.

There was general laughter before Julia continued. "What I mean by a 'silliness quotient' is that the teachers let the kids be kids. Many children are funny. They say odd things, laugh at inappropriate times, sing with abandon. I always liked teachers who enjoyed us for being kids, rather than those who tried to turn us into mini-adults."

There were some murmurs among the mothers before Mylan continued, "You see? We all look for different qualities, whether it's those you already mentioned or others like ethics, character, joie de vivre, flexibility, or even authoritarianism."

"Right on!" Julia volunteered. "And if your kids 'can't get no satisfaction,' she said, referring to the Rolling Stones song, "you transfer them, but only 'if you try, you try, you try, you trrrrry . . .'"

By then the entire group, except Constance, started singing a medley of Rolling Stones songs, and the subject of teachers was soon forgotten.

All these years later I still remember my own kindergarten teacher. She was kind and gentle and made us all feel loved. My kids have been equally lucky even though we've moved twice and our two girls attended kindergarten in different schools.

Johnna, mother of Madelaine, 9, and Zoe, 15

An Art, Not a Science

Larry Cuban, Ph.D., is a professor of education at Stanford University.

What are the qualities of a good teacher?

It depends on whom you talk to and what they want from a kindergarten program. Parents and educators would generally agree that the best teachers understand and like children. They respond to them in an affectionate and warm manner, and they value and encourage creativity. Devotion, conscientiousness, and communication skills are important as well. Most early childhood educators would add the following professional expertise. They would want someone who

- understands the broad range of intellectual, emotional, and social developmental issues that affect kindergarten-age children

- recognizes that each child is different and is willing to teach to children's strengths and weaknesses

- plans and organizes tasks and activities that encourage all children to explore new boundaries and to apply and practice what they learn

- facilitates relationships among children as they learn to work together in small and large groups

For good reason, there may be some dissension between parents' and teachers' definition of professional expertise. What may account for the differences is that parents are concerned about their individual son or daughter and a kindergarten teacher is concerned about a group of fifteen to twenty-five students. Parents and teachers may differ, among themselves and between each other, over the purpose of kindergarten. Should the top priority be to academically prepare children for first grade? Or to help each child grow intellectually, emotionally, and socially, even if such growth is unconnected to learning to read, manage numbers, and boot up a computer. The answer is an assimilation of both goals. The emphasis will depend upon the teacher's beliefs and values as well as those of her principal. Of course they will also reflect school district and state educational policies.

Is good teaching an art or a science?

Professional expertise can be acquired. Kindergarten teachers can learn how children develop intellectually, emotionally, and socially. They can be taught to understand the complexities of how children learn a concept or develop a skill. They can learn how to organize activities that are appropriate for each child's stage of development.

Personal characteristics, as well as values and beliefs, differ among people. They can be taught but seldom learned. A teacher's ability to instill among her students a love of learning, a lifelong curiosity, and a sense of personal achievement is an art, not a science.

I think a kindergarten teacher can determine whether a child begins feeling good about her- or himself, or doesn't. Unfortunately, there were so many rules in my son's class that he was afraid to go to school. We changed teachers during the second month of school, and Bart became a new child.

Rene, mother of
Bart, 7

Teaching Kinders

Sherry Kaufman has taught kindergarten for twenty-five years, and Sandra Chon Wang has taught kindergarten for ten. They are both teachers at Westwood Charter Elementary School in Los Angeles, California.

Kindergarten is a unique opportunity for a teacher to establish a solid foundation for the rest of a child's school career. It sets the tone of what school is all about. Often, we begin the year emphasizing to children that "just like your moms and dads have their jobs, your job is to come to school every day and to do your very best work."

One of the most enjoyable aspects of teaching kindergartners is working with the developmental levels of five- and six-year-olds. Children at this age are honest, sincere, and willing to tell you about every aspect of their lives. In other

I personally thought I'd like more experienced teachers who have seen everything and dealt with it. Two of my kids had older teachers and one had a teacher who'd taught only for two years. I learned that age doesn't make any difference. Enthusiasm and a love of children does.

Carmen, mother of
Ana, 6, Sawyer, 8,
and Enrique, 11

words, that means we teachers know every detail of your family's personal lives. Consider them mini-CIA agents who are willing to report anything to their fearless leader (their kindergarten teacher). Nothing is sacred to kindergartners.

One of the perks of being a kindergarten teacher (or supreme being) is that you are never wrong. Parents often inform us that their directions have now been overridden by those of the teacher. They tell us that the children now chime in at home, "But Ms. Smith said I should do it this way."

The funny insights and interpretations that come out of children's mouths make us laugh often and hard. One teacher remembers a morning when her class was reciting the "Pledge of Allegiance" and she overheard a student say, "And to the republic, for Richard stands."

Successful kindergarten teachers understand the developmental level of five- to six-year-olds. There is often a wide range in social and academic levels. The biggest obstacle at the beginning of the year is helping children make the transition from a small preschool environment that emphasized social activities to a structured environment where children are held accountable and asked to be independent. The biggest hurdle in this transitional period is separation anxiety. It can be experienced by parents as well as children. We have strategies for both. For parents, we send them off for a cup of coffee with a package of tissues and the reassurance that their child will be fine. For children, we use a variety of approaches. For example, we have the child sit close to us or pair them with a special buddy; we might have them write a letter expressing their feelings and have them sign it; we might draw a clock to show what time their parent(s) will arrive; or we have parents pack pictures, letters, or familiar objects in the child's backpack so the child may look at them throughout the day. Often what we find is that children's anxiety only lasts a few minutes (whereas the parents' lasts until pickup time). We try to remind parents to talk about how well the child's day went with him or her so that the child begins to feel secure about returning to school the following day.

Over the past few years, one of the observations that we have made as kindergarten teachers is that children are coming into kindergarten with more readiness skills and more sophisticated information about the world than ever before. The challenge in teaching kindergarten today is striking a balance between maintaining a developmentally appropriate program that incorporates play as a vehicle for learning and presenting information that is rich in content and challenging to children from all learning levels who enter our kindergarten classroom.

Testing

I never tested well, and I'm a college professor.

Tandra, mother of Calvin, 7, and Kathy, 9

"How do you feel about kindergarten readiness testing?" I asked Marshall, a friend who teaches preschool.

"To be quite honest," he replied, "I don't understand it."

"What do you mean?"

"I've been teaching preschool for ten years. Everyone knows that testing is not the best way to determine a child's intelligence or ability."

"So why are children tested?" I asked.

"At our school, they are tested only if they're going on to private school, which is about a third of our graduating kindergarten class. I imagine in less affluent socioeconomic areas, where the children may not have attended preschool, they may be tested for public school as well. Anyway the private schools test, whether it's developmentally appropriate or not. And they test in different ways."

"How?"

"A few of the more progressive schools test the children by watching them play," Marshall replied.

"I am having a difficult time trying to figure out the criteria for being an 'outstanding player,'" I facetiously said. "Might it have something to do with sharing toys, not throwing sand, and demonstrating a certain amount of creativity?"

"That's a fairly accurate assessment of sandbox play, but there's also jumping, skipping, tricycle riding, and other motor development skills. And you're forgetting 'inside' play, which at our school is almost everything else we do."

"You mean like cutting, pasting, drawing, building with blocks, stuff like that?"

"Yeah. Also storytelling."

"Which is probably very telling," I said, admiring my own play on words.

"It is particularly interesting if children know they are going to be tested, and the parents have tutored them."

"About being naughty or nice?" I asked.

"Same idea and probably the same reward," Marshall responded. "If you do this well, we'll buy you a present."

"Marshall, I have to object to that value judgment. Since you are not a parent, I realize you don't know that in certain situations, bribery is actually a fairly effective parenting tool," I suggested.

He gave me one of those looks. I shrugged my shoulders.

"They will direct their child not to tell stories about action adventure figures, characters in inappropriate films they've taken their kids to, or sibling rivalry issues."

"You mean children should not make up stories about wonderful storks who take their infant brother or sister back from whence they came."

"Something like that," he answered. "And using bathroom words as adjectives is a no-no."

"Probably a good idea," I mused. "So tell me about academic testing."

"It's more common. There is all the kindergarten readiness stuff you hear about. The kids are given these little workbooks and suddenly expected to know how to fill in squares or bubbles or whatever. To add to their level of stress, many parents tell their children they will be tested, so the kids are already apprehensive. Some parents either do home preparation or send them to mini-SAT training camps."

"That sure makes childhood seem like a playful time," I responded. "Bet these kids can't wait for kindergarten."

"Yeah, right," Marshall responded with sarcasm. "Of course, the other side of all this is the personal interview."

"Kind of like a college admission interview?"

"Yeah, except you've got to remember we're talking about four- or five-year-olds."

"So, how can you train a kid of this age to interview?" I naively asked.

"Eye contact is key, and so is smiling."

"But if they smile too much, won't they look idiotic?"

"There's a fine line," Marshall responded. "Figuring it out takes a certain level of sophisticated judgment on their part."

"Sure sounds like it."

"You also want your child to be polite. He or she must understand that it's not a good idea to make funny faces, sing, or prance around."

"That sounds a little rigid to me," I said.

He ignored me and continued with a sigh. "Finally, you must teach them how to answer questions in a thoughtful yet direct manner."

"Wow," I slowly said. "I wonder how many adults could pass the test."

"Gives you pause for doubt, doesn't it?"

> *We did a lot of test preparation at home. It made all the difference.*
>
> Stuart, father of Brianna, 6, and Laurie, 8

Testing

Samuel J. Meisels, Ed.D., is a professor of education at the University of Michigan and the author of *Developmental Screening in Early Childhood: A Guide.*

What is the value of standardized testing in kindergarten?

Standardized testing is valuable for certain purposes. Every child entering kindergarten should go through a valid and reliable fifteen-minute developmental screening test as a means of identifying those children who may have special needs. Children who do not do well on the developmental screening test need further evaluation. No decisions about whether a child has special needs can be made from a screening alone. This is an example of a valuable standardized test.

Prior to the beginning of school, readiness tests are often used to determine whether children are prepared for kindergarten, but research confirms that children may do poorly on these tests simply because they have not had the opportunity to learn what is on the tests, rather than because they are incapable of learning. The children who don't do well on readiness tests are the ones who *need* to be in kindergarten. I strongly oppose these tests if they are used to decide who should go to kindergarten because they have no predictive powers.

Achievement tests are those that parents read about in newspapers. They are used in many places to establish school ratings. Every state has a test of one sort or another, few of which are administered before third grade. Some states and school districts use similar tests, produced by commercial test manufacturers, such as the Iowa Test of Basic Skills and the California Achievement Test (CAT). These tests have little value for parents, teachers, and policy makers, let alone for children. They tell us very little about what a child is learning.

How are achievement tests administered to kindergartners?

Achievement tests and readiness tests record what a child has learned in various curricular domains, such as math, reading, or science. Achievement tests are typically administered in a group format, which is a problem for many children. Researchers have found that when five- and six-year-olds are asked to sit for extended periods, even if that time is parceled in half-hour segments, kids do what you would expect them to do. They get out of their seats, call out the answers, and bop each other on the head. Sometimes teachers who administer pretests are supposed to repeat the instructions if children are not listening, but may forget to do so.

After two weeks of testing, my daughter came home with a stomachache every day. I thought I would get an ulcer.

Mark, father of Victoria, 6, and Drew, 9

Ironically, standardized testing is intended to be "objective" but is, in fact, highly nonobjective. It is not an accurate predictor of future success. Teaching and learning records and observationally based assessments are much more accurate. Moreover, there is a great deal of test preparation or teaching to the test.

These test preparation programs are designed to teach children how to find rows and columns and fill in bubbles and they also focus on the tests' content. When the teacher shows children a page in a booklet and says, "Look for the row that has a picture of a bird on it," they will quickly find the row the teacher is talking about. The problem with this is that the children's scores may go up on tests because of this kind of preparation, but this will not mean that the child *knows* more. Rather, the child simply has been taught what is on the test.

What effect does test taking have on kindergartners?

Children quickly learn that there are consequences for performing well or poorly on these tests. They also find for the first time that the rules have changed in their classroom. Previously it was okay to ask questions if you did not understand something, to get out of your seat, and work cooperatively with others. The teacher was there to support the child; to be his or her partner in learning. But in a test situation, children suddenly are expected to sit still and work alone. It becomes a cognitively discrepant and unpleasant experience for children.

What should parents know about testing?

What's key for parents to know is that achievement and readiness tests often may not reflect what your child knows or is capable of doing. Whether he or she does well or not, the results of these tests are nothing to be excited about. No single test administered on one occasion is going to tell you what your child knows, and many teachers are aware this is not the answer to how your child is doing in school. Talk to your children. Find out what they are learning. Talk to your children's teacher and discuss their progress. Remember that most of those tests cannot accurately assess your child's achievement. You do not want your child to be made a victim of a policy that is not well informed or child-friendly.

Fortunately, there is not a great deal of achievement testing in kindergarten but there is a fair amount of readiness testing. A better tool is a performance assessment, which is a method I use to help teachers observe children's work and their learning. Teachers can keep track and evaluate progress and then feed back information to parents about how their children are doing across the entire year. More and more school districts and states are using this kind of assessment in place of conventional testing. A performance assessment informs the teacher about each child's progress so that the teacher can see the strengths and areas of weakness of each child and can thereby adjust the curriculum. It enhances teaching and results in improving learning.

As far as I'm concerned, it's a good thing. The children are being prepared for the first grade and it's important to know where they stand.

Marla, mother of Morgan, 7, and Elyse, 9

Writing

My daughter has great penmanship. As far as I'm concerned, it's like having good table manners. It will bode well for her for the rest of her life.

Larry, father of
Adrienne, 6

"Andre learned to print in preschool," his father James told me on the telephone. "I wasn't sure it was a good idea. His numbers and letters were poorly formed. My wife, Marilyn, asked me how well I'd write if I had to use a crayon," James said, with a slight laugh. "She had a point, but I told her I didn't remember our older children learning to write when they were so young. Marilyn told me that times had changed.

"I talked to the preschool director, who told me that learning to write the letters of the alphabet is an important cognitive step connecting oral speech and written language. In other words, writing would help Andre learn to read. I wasn't sure I agreed, but when Marilyn asked me if I had secretly gotten a teaching credential, I backed off.

"As far as I could see, kindergarten was an extension of the preschool mind-set. Andre started writing, if you call it that, in a journal. After two weeks, when he brought home his journal to show us his accomplishments, I was stunned. He was so proud, but what he wrote was gibberish with some drawings and letters tossed in.

"Marilyn told me to 'chill out,' but the next day I made an appointment with his teacher, Mr. Skandera. As I sat down,

216

I noticed he had a folder with Andre's name on the desk in front of him. After we dispensed with the preliminaries I said, 'Mr. Skandera, I know times have changed since my older children went to school. They didn't learn how to write until the first grade. But when they did, the letters were modeled on the blackboard. They practiced over and over until each letter was neatly and legibly written. I find it difficult to believe that the quality of Andre's work is acceptable.'"

"'Mr. Tigner,' he replied with a smile, 'I've been teaching kindergarten for twenty-one years, and you're right. We teach differently from the ways we once did. Years ago a group of educational researchers determined that the earlier children learn to write, the easier it will be for them to read.'

"'But what about the quality of their printing?' I asked.

"'That comes later. What's important is that from day one, children begin seeing themselves as writers. They write or talk about what they know. They feel good about their accomplishments. Let me show you something.'

"We got up, walked over to one of the classroom computers, and sat down on those tiny chairs. Mr. Skandera inserted a disk of a reading program and demonstrated how it worked. He explained how children, working in pairs, sit at a computer and respond to questions posed by a synthesized voice. They are instructed to type and say sounds or words.

"'I've never heard of that,' I said.

"'It's fairly common now. The value of this kind of instruction, together with journal writing and dictation—children make up stories that adults type—enables us to present the written and spoken word in so many ways.'

"'I never thought of it that way.'

"'In the old days, by the end of kindergarten, children could write about ten words or more. Now that they are able to speak and write words, the number of words to which they are exposed has increased exponentially.'

"I left that day with a totally different perception of the writing and reading process. When Andre came home at the

My kids' writing stinks. I figure they can all be doctors.

Norm, father of
Jill, 7, Bonnie, 9,
and Eldon, 11

end of the week with his journal, I asked him to explain what he had written. I was amazed by what the squiggles meant."

Successful Writing

Patricia Deck is coauthor of *Success in Reading and Writing*. She has been project director of The Learning Circle in Guilford County, North Carolina, and an education program specialist for the Southeastern Regional Vision for Education.

What does a good kindergarten writing program encompass?

In kindergarten we are concerned with students learning about letters and developing a phonemic awareness of what sounds and letters represent. As this evolution occurs, we encourage them to connect reading with writing.

Early writing is often drawing pictures, telling a story, and retelling the story. When children sit down at a table and scribble, they think of themselves as writers. The desire to write starts early and should be encouraged. In the classroom, teachers should give children a daily opportunity to choose to write as a free-time activity. This is in addition to the writing the teacher may plan in response to a book read or as follow-up to an activity the class has completed. For example, if the class has taken a field trip to the zoo or grocery store, the children might write about their experience. If they are studying a certain letter and its sound, the students might write words they know with that letter or copy words they can find in the classroom that have that letter.

When children write in response to reading, it is usually retelling the story or expanding the ideas of a story in their own words. Children should also be able to "read"—understand and explain—their own writing. It is important for children to know that reading and writing are connected. They develop together and they both require thinking. We want children to read and reflect on what they read, draw conclusions, and make predictions. Both their reading and writing skills improve through writing. Writing helps clarify thinking.

What is the progression in learning to write?

First children draw pictures. Then they scribble because to them that looks like writing. Sometimes they will draw a picture and put a letter with it, or they will combine scribbles with actual letters. In kindergarten, teachers start helping children learn to form the letters. They teach children to hear sounds. When they start school, the kids are encouraged to write words. At some point, teachers will write or type stories the children relate to them. When children learn to write their own stories, they tend to use temporary spelling. They write the letters they think represent the words they use.

As the children read more and their vocabularies grow, they will incorporate more words into their writing. As they are able to write about their own lives, school activities, or books their teacher has read, their writing will improve. You learn to write by writing, so children's writing improves as they are able to have more real and authentic opportunities to do so. With a growing awareness of how writing communicates thoughts and ideas and as their confidence grows and they experience positive responses to their writing, most children will want to learn to spell words correctly to be able to communicate their ideas and thoughts more easily.

Teachers can use techniques such as word walls to help students learn to spell the most frequently used words. Parents can reinforce this by writing words their child may ask them to spell on pieces of paper or index cards and display them for the child to use as a spelling reference.

What can parents do to help their children develop writing skills?

Parents need to understand the importance of talking to their children at an early age. Children who are read to and talked to from birth are more language-aware. They begin to understand the relationship between talking, reading, and writing. In homes where there is neither conversation nor any exchange about thoughts, feelings, or activities, children most likely will have delayed language development.

Parents can also help their kindergartners learn to understand the relationship between the words children hear and those they see. When you are reading to your child, it is important to point out words as you read them. Relate words to common objects. Pick up a cereal box and read what's on the box. As you walk around your neighborhood, read street signs and address numbers. When you're shopping, read names of stores. These activities teach children about the relationship between print and meaning.

When you are reading aloud to your children, talk with them about stories. Tell them how books are written, how an author might think about an idea for a story and write it. Explain how the pictures and words are printed and bound into a book that you can read. Ask your children why they think the author wrote the story you are reading and what they might write about in their own stories. Again, you are pointing out the connection between print and reading.

A word of advice: Parents should not be so concerned about their children's reading and writing development, but rather, observe and support their interests. Follow their lead. Read aloud to your child every day, rather than placing him or her in front of the television set. Talk about what you are reading. Encourage your children to write thank-you notes when they receive gifts. If they don't want your help writing these notes, don't offer it. Children need to develop confidence in their own abilities, and if you proofread what they write, criticize it, or comment on their penmanship, you are not helping them.

If there are other children in your child's class who need individualized help or tutoring, consider volunteering to help in the classroom. Realize that you are not only helping that child, but also by your very presence you are letting all the children know how much you value reading and writing.

*W*ho needs to learn to write in kindergarten? Honestly!

Caroline, mother of Martin, 7, and Jeannie, 9

What skills should children acquire by the end of the year?

When learning to read and write, children learn the names of the letters, the shapes, and the sounds. Once they have mastered letter recognition and they understand the relationship between words and printed material, they often begin reading, as if it were magic. It is difficult to say what skills a child should know by the end of kindergarten, because all children do not begin kindergarten with the same background for understanding written language in their lives. We can say that it should be expected that all children would know the letters in their own names, be able to print those letters and use those letters in their writing. Children should perceive themselves as writers and understand that print conveys meaning. Using both picture symbols and letters or combinations of the two, most kindergarten children should be able to retell stories or experiences, write notes of observation and ideas, and read their compositions.

Nothing is more exciting than to see young children scrambling for the "author's chair" in their classroom to read their compositions or to have the experience of publishing their first book. This newfound means of expressing themselves is a foundation from which all other learning proceeds. Parents should never expect or accept less than their child becoming comfortable as a reader and a writer.

Zen of Kindergarten

"Why is kindergarten such a big deal" I asked my friend Gracie who'd been an educational researcher before becoming a botanist.

She paused, then said, "Kindergarten sets the tone for children's school careers. If it's a good experience, they become excited about school. If it's not, they begin tuning out or doubting their abilities."

"At five or six years old?" I asked, with surprise.

"Yes," she simply replied. "And for parents it's the beginning of their kids' formal education. Kindergarten evaluations are part of the cumulative record children take with them through high school."

"Right," I said, with a laugh. "Kindergarten is the first step in the pathway to college."

"We both know parents who feel that way. It's a typical left-brain response; one I might have expected from you had you not 'flipped out'."

"I would not categorize a focus on the emotional side of the kindergarten experience as 'flipping out'," I defensively responded. "I must admit it was unusual that I did not approach the subject in an analytical way. It was out of character that for a nine-month period, I felt like I was on a roller-coaster ride and that the attendant with the key had vanished," I freely admitted. "It was curious that I handled the experience in a less mature fashion than Alex," I mused.

"And to what would you attribute your quirky little behavioral pattern?"

"The trauma of kindergarten," I said. "I was unprepared. Nobody told me what to expect. The first day of school I had such a huge case of separation anxiety that when Alex left the auditorium for his classroom, I could barely breathe. Luckily I didn't have to leave him at school; we were separated for only one half-hour. The second day, after he followed his teacher into the building and waved good-bye, I bolted, ran to my car, and started sobbing."

Gracie seemed at a loss for words.

"A few weeks later, tears came to my eyes when I saw the first notation Alex made in his journal."

"What did he write?"

"*a.*"

"The letter *a*?"

"Yes. Then *b*, a backward *l*, and so on. And his teacher stamped her sign of approval on all his papers."

"Stamped?"

"You know, a rubber stamp with written phrases like, 'radical reader,' 'awesome,' 'great job'; picture stamps with a happy face, red lips that mean hugs and kisses, a smiling bear, a shark whose caption reads 'sharp,' a penguin with a pen writing the words 'first class.'"

"And this made you cry?"

"Yeah."

"Why?"

I shrugged.

"Jeez, I didn't realize the level of your adjustment problems. Why didn't you tell me?"

"I think I tried but you seemed to be busy—for an entire year."

"Undoubtedly with good reason," she replied with a chuckle. "Dare I ask if there's anything more you'd like to share with me?"

"With that attitude, I won't tell you about the absorbing field trips, moving holiday parties, stimulating open house, or the poignant graduation ceremony," I said.

"Puhleese!"

"Gracie, it's your loss, not mine. Other than childbirth [Gracie is the mother of an infant son] kindergarten is one of the most extraordinary experiences I have encountered as a parent. The natural instinct—to protect one's child from harm, to provide for his well-being, to ensure that she flourishes—is overpowering. Just wait until Justin is older."

"I'm not as emotional as you are."

"Be that as it may, given your first Ph.D. is in education, I really can't understand your disinterest."

"Educational statistics is as far afield from teaching as botany is from gardening."

"But surely you see the similarity between your two chosen professions."

"If you start discussing Friedrich Froebel, the child's garden, planting seeds, and watching them grow, I truly am going to drop you as a friend," Gracie said.

I smiled like a Zen master; she rolled her eyeballs. When I started singing "God Bless the Child," we both burst into laughter.

Appendix

Signs of a Good Kindergarten Classroom

Kindergarten is a time for children to expand their love of learning, their general knowledge, their ability to get along with others, and their interest in reaching out to the world. While kindergarten marks an important transition from preschool to the primary grades, it is important that children still get to be children—getting kindergartners ready for elementary school does not mean substituting academics for playtime, forcing children to master first grade "skills," or relying on standardized tests to assess children's success. Kindergarten "curriculum" actually includes such events as snack time, recess, and individual and group activities in addition to those activities we think of as traditionally educational.

Developmentally appropriate kindergarten classrooms encourage the growth of children's self-esteem, their cultural identities, their independence, and their individual strengths. Kindergarten children will continue to develop control of their own behavior through the guidance and support of warm, caring adults. At this stage, children possess an innate curiosity and are already ready to learn. Teachers with a strong background in early childhood education and child development can best provide for children what they need to grow physically, emotionally, and intellectually. The following are signs of a good kindergarten classroom.

1. Children are playing and working with materials or other children. They do not wander aimlessly, and they are not expected to sit quietly for long periods of time.

2. Children have access to various activities throughout the day, such as block building, pretend play, picture books, paints and other art materials, and table toys such as matching games, pegboards, and puzzles. Children are not all doing the same thing at the same time.

3. Teachers work with individual children, small groups, and the whole group at different times. They do not spend all their time with the entire group.

4. The classroom is decorated with children's original artwork, their own writing with invented spelling, and dictated stories.

5. Children learn numbers and the alphabet in the context of their everyday experiences. Exploring the natural world of plants and animals, cooking, taking attendance, and serving the snack are all meaningful activities to children.

6. Children work on projects and have long periods of time (at least an hour) to play and explore. Filling out worksheets should not be their primary activity.

7. Children have an opportunity to play outside every day that weather permits. This play is never sacrificed for instructional time.

8. Teachers read books to children throughout the day, not just at group story time.

9. Curriculum is adapted for those who are ahead as well as those who need additional help. Because children dif-

fer in experiences and background, they do not learn the same things at the same time in the same way.

10. Children and their parents look forward to school. Parents feel safe about sending their child to the program. Children are happy to attend; they do not cry regularly or complain of feeling sick.

11. Individual kindergarten classrooms will vary, and curriculum will vary according to the interests and backgrounds of the children. But all developmentally appropriate kindergarten classrooms will have one thing in common; the focus will be on the development of the child as a whole.

Resources

- -

Books of Interest

Ames, Louise Bates, and Frances L. Ilg
  Your Four-Year-Old: Wild and Wonderful (Dell, 1981)

Ames, Louise Bates, Frances L. Ilg, and Betty David
  Your Five-Year-Old: Sunny and Serene (Dell, 1981)
  Your Six-Year-Old: Loving and Defiant (Dell, 1981)

Balter, Lawrence, and Catherine Tamis-Lemonda, editors
  Child Psychology: A Handbook of Contemporary Issues (Pyschology Press, 1999)

Banks, James A.
  Multicultural Education: Issues and Perspectives (John Wiley & Sons, 1999)
  Educating Citizens in a Multicultural Society (Teachers College Press, 1997)

Banner, James M. Jr., and Harold C. Cannon
  The Elements of Teaching (Yale University Press, 1997)

Bettelheim, Bruno
  A Good Enough Parent (Vintage Books, 1987)

Bettelheim, Bruno, with Karen Zelan
  On Learning to Read (Knopf, 1992)

Bloom, Jill
   Help Me to Help My Child: A Source-book for Parents of Learning Disabled Children (Little, Brown and Company, 1990)

Briggs, Dorothy Corville
   Your Child's Self-Esteem (Doubleday, 1965)

Brunner, Cornelia, and William Tally
   The New Media Literacy Handbook: An Educators Guide to Bringing New Media into the Classroom (Anchor Books, 1999)

Brunner, Jerome
   The Process of Education (Harvard University Press, 1962)

Caplan, Theresa and Frank
   The Early Childhood Years: The 2- to 6-Year-Old (Bantam Books, 1984)

Clements, Douglas, C., Alan Reidesel, and James E. Schwartz
   Teaching Elementary School Mathematics (Allyn & Bacon, 1996)

Comer, James
   Child by Child: The Comer Process for Change in Education (Teachers College Press, 2000)

Cummins, Paul F., and Anna K. Cummins
   For Mortal Stakes: Solutions for Schools and Society (Peter Lang Publishing, 1998)

Domash, Leanne, with Judith Sachs
   Wanna Be My Friend? How to Strengthen Your Child's Social Skills (Hearst Books, 1999)

Elkind, David
   Miseducation: Preschoolers at Risk (Knopf, 1992)
   The Hurried Child: Growing Up Too Fast Too Soon (Addison-Wesley, 1981)

Fisher, Bobbi
   Joyful Learning in Kindergarten (Heinemann, 1998)

Gardner, Howard
   Creating Minds (Basic Books, 1993)
   Multiple Intelligences: The Theory in Practice (Basic Books, 1993)

Graves, Michael, Bonnie Graves, and Susan M. Watts-Taffe
   Essentials of Elementary Reading (Allyn & Bacon, 1998)

Graves, Michael, Connie Juel, and Bonnie Graves
   Teaching Reading in the 21st Century (Allyn & Bacon, 1998)

Greenspan, Stanley I., M.D., with
Jacqueline Salmon
    *Playground Politics: Understanding the
    Emotional Life of Your School-Age
    Child* (Addison-Wesley, 1993)

Griffith, Mary
    *The Unschooling Handbook: How to Use
    the Whole World as Your Child's Class-
    room* (Prima Communications, 1998)

Griffith, Mary, and Lisa Cooper
    *The Homeschooling Handbook: From
    Preschool to High School, a Parent's
    Guide* (Prima Communications,
    1999)

Hall, Susan L., and Louise C. Moats
    *Straight Talk About Reading: How Par-
    ents Can Make a Difference During the
    Early Years* (Contemporary Books,
    1999)

Healy, Jane
    *Failure to Connect: How Computers Affect
    Our Children's Minds—and What We
    Can Do About It* (Touchstone, 1999)

Hirsch, E. D., and John Holdren
    *What Your Kindergartner Needs to Know:
    Preparing Your Child for a Lifetime of
    Learning* (Doubleday, 1996)

Holt, John
    Freedom and Beyond (Heinemann, 1995)
    How Children Learn (Perseus Press,
    1995)

Katz, Lilian
    Talks with Teachers of Young Children
    (Ablex Publishing, 1995)

Katz, Lilian, and Sylvia C. Chard
    *Engaging Children's Minds: The Project
    Approach* (Ablex Publishing, 1995)

Kay, Alan
    "Computers, Networks, and Educa-
    tion" (*Scientific American,* 1991, Vol.
    265, no. 3)

Koetzsch, Ronald E.
    *The Parents' Guide to Alternatives in
    Education* (Shambahala, 1997)

Kurcinka, Mary Sheedy
    Raising Your Spirited Child (Harper
    Perennial, 1991)

Lillard, Paula Polk
    *Montessori Today: A Comprehensive
    Approach to Education from Birth to
    Adulthood* (Schocken, 1996)

Meisels, Samuel
    *Developmental Screening in Early Child-
    hood: A Guide* (National Association
    for the Education of Young Chil-
    dren, 1994)

Meisels, Samuel, and Jack P. Shonkoff,
editors
    Handbook of Early Childhood Intervention
    (Cambridge University Press, 1998)

Morrison, George S.
  Early Childhood Education Today
    (Prentice-Hall, 1998)

Nathan, Joe
  *Charter Schools: Creating Hope and
    Opportunity for American Education*
    (Jossey-Bass Publishers, 1996)

Papert, Seymour
  *Mindstorms, Children, Computers, and
    Powerful Ideas* (Basic Books, 1993)

Perrone, Vito
  *101 Educational Conversations with Your
    Kindergartner–First Grader* (Chelsea
    House Publishers, 1993)

Piaget, Jean
  The Origins of Intelligence in Children
    (International Universities Press,
    1952)

Postman, Neil
  *The End of Education: Redefining the
    Value of School* (Vintage Books, 1996)

Rosenberg, Michael, Lawrence O'Shea,
and Dorothy O'Shea
  *Student Teacher to Master Teacher: A
    Practical Guide for Educating Students
    with Special Needs* (Prentice Hall,
    1997)

Salk, Lee
  *Familyhood: Nurturing the Values That
    Matter* (Simon & Schuster, 1992)

Shalway, Linda
  *Learning to Teach . . . Not Just for Begin-
    ners: The Essential Guide for All
    Teachers* (Scholastic Professional
    Books, 1998)

Singer, Jerome, and Dorothy G. Singer
  *The House of Make-Believe: Children's
    Play and the Developing Imagination*
    (Harvard University Press, 1992)

Tapscott, Don
  *Growing Up Digital: The Rise of the Net
    Generation* (McGraw-Hill, 1998)

Trelease, Jim
  The New Read-Aloud Handbook
    (Penguin Books, 1989)

Unger, Harlow W.
  How to Pick a Perfect Private School
    (Checkmark Books, 1999)

Wood, George
  A Time to Learn (Penguin, 1999)
  *Schools That Work: America's Most Inno-
    vative Public Education Programs*
    (Dutton, 1993)

Zigler, Edward, and Matia Finn-Stevenson
  *Schools of the 21st Century: Linking
    Child Care and Education* (Westview
    Press, 1999)

Zigler, Edward, and Susan Muenchow
  *Head Start: The Inside Story of America's
    Most Successful Educational Experiment*
    (Basic Books, 1994)

Organizations

- -

AAHPERD, the American Alliance of Health, Physical Education, Recreation, and Dance, which includes the Council on Physical Education for Children, is the largest organization of professionals supporting and assisting those involved in physical education, leisure, fitness, dance, health promotion, and education.

    1900 Association Drive
    Reston, Virginia, 20191
    Phone: (800) 213-7193; (703) 476-3400
    Website: www.aahperd.org

Core Knowledge Foundation, founded by E. D. Hirsch Jr., provides a model of education in which each and every student would follow a grade-by-grade sequence of specific guidelines in history, geography, mathematics, science, language arts, and the fine arts—and thus develop a core of shared knowledge.

    Website: www.coreknowledge.org
    E-mail: coreknow@coreknowledge.org

ERIC, the Educational Resources Information Center Clearinghouse on Elementary and Early Childhood Education, is a national information center funded by the U.S. Department of Education through the department's Office of Educational Research and Improvement. It is an extraordinary source of information. They provide ERIC sites, resources, a search ERIC database, and more. Lilian G. Katz, the director, is a nationally known educator and professor emerita at the University of Illinois at Urbana-Champaign.

    ERIC Clearinghouse on Elementary
       and Early Childhood Education
       (ERIC/EECE)
    University of Illinois at Urbana-
       Champaign
    Children's Research Center
    51 Gerty Drive
    Champaign, IL 61820-7469
    Phone: (800) 583-4135; (217) 333-1386
    Fax: (217) 333-3767
    Website: www.ericeece.org
    E-mail: ericeece@uiuc.edu

Growing Without Schooling is the website for John Holt's bookstore, which specializes in tools and ideas for independent learning. Holt, educational innovator and author of *How Children Learn*, *How Children Fail*, and *Freedom and Beyond* (among other books), was a school reformer, unschooling reformer, and a pioneer in the homeschooling movement. This site provides a plethora of materials and links to other homeschooling sites.

    John Holt's Bookstore
    2380 Massachusetts Avenue, Suite 104
    Cambridge, MA 02140-1226
    Phone: (617) 864-3100
    Fax: (617) 864-9235
    Website: www.holtgws.com

Kathy Schrock's Guide for Educators is a categorized list of sites useful for enhancing curriculum and professional growth. It is updated daily to include the best sites for teaching and learning.

    Website: www.discoveryschool.com
    E-mail: kschrock@capecod.net

NAEA, the National Art Education Association, promotes art through professional development, service, advancement of knowledge, and leadership.

    1916 Association Drive
    Reston, VA 20191
    Phone: (703) 860-8000
    Fax: (703) 860-2960
    Website: www.naea-reston.org

NAEYC, the National Association for the Education of Young Children, is the nation's largest organization of early childhood professionals and others dedicated to the quality of children's early education. The association administers a voluntary, national accreditation system for high-quality early childhood programs and publishes an extensive array of books, brochures, videotapes, and posters for parents and professionals. If you wish to receive the free brochure "A Good Kindergarten for Your Child," send a self-addressed, stamped envelope to NAEYC.

    1509 16th Street NW (Box 524)
    Washington, DC 20036
    Phone: (800) 424-2460; (202) 232-8777
    Website: www.naeyc.org

NAIS, the National Association of Independent Schools, represents more than 1,100 independent schools, maintains a researchable database of independent schools, including details on admissions, financial aid, and workshops for teachers and administrators.

    1620 L Street NW
    Washington, DC 20036-6505
    Phone: (202) 973-9700
    Fax: (202) 973-9790
    Website: www.nais.org

NCBE, the National Clearinghouse for Bilingual Education, is funded by the U.S. Department of Education's Office of Bilingual Education and Minority Languages Affairs to collect, analyze, and disseminate information relating to the effective education of linguistically and culturally diverse learners in the United States. NCBE is operated by the George Washington University Center for the Study of Language and Education.

    2011 Eye Street NW, Suite 200
    Washington, DC 20006
    Phone: (800) 531-9347; (202) 467-0867
    Website: www.ncbe.gwu.edu
    E-mail: askncbe@ncbe.gwu.edu

NCSS, the National Council for the Social Studies, contributed an abridged version of their position statement, "Social Studies for Early Childhood and Elementary School Children: Preparing for the 21st Century." The full text of the position paper can be found on the NCSS website: www.socialstudies.org under the heading *Standards and Position Statements.*

3501 Newark Street NW
Washington, DC 20016
Phone: (202) 966-7840

NCTM, the National Council of Teachers of Mathematics, is dedicated to improving mathematics teaching and learning from preschool through postsecondary school.

1906 Association Drive
Reston, VA 20191
Phone: (703) 620-9840
Fax: (703) 476-2970
Website: www.nctm.org
E-mail: nctm@nctm.org

NEA, the National Education Association, is America's oldest and largest organization committed to advancing the cause of public education.

1201 16th Street NW
Washington, DC 20036
Phone: (202) 833-4000
Website: www.nea.org

NECTAS, the National Early Childhood Technical Assistance System, at the University of North Carolina's National Early Childhood Technical Assistance program refers the parents of learning disabled children to programs of the Individuals with Disabilities Act.

137 East Franklin Street, Suite 500
Chapel Hill, NC 27514
Phone: (919) 962-2001;
     TDD: (877) 574-3194
Fax: (919) 966-7463
Website: www.nectas.unc.edu
E-mail: nectas@unc.edu

NICHCY, the National Information Center for Children and Youth with Disabilities, is a service of the U.S. Department of Education. Their website provides extensive resources and referrals to organizations and programs servicing learning-disabled families and their children.

P.O. Box 1492
Washington, DC 20013-1492
Phone: (800) 695-0285;
     Voice/TTY (202) 884-8200
Website: www.nichcy.org

NPIN, the National Parent Information Network, is a project of the ERIC system. They provide articles on a wide variety of subjects through their Virtual Library, or you can do an individual search and more.

NPIN Website: http://npin.org

NRCG/T, the National Center on the Gifted and Talented, whose director is Dr. Joseph S. Renzulli, plans and carries out research on students with high abilities. They place emphasis on identifying the research needs of economically disadvantaged youth, individuals of limited English proficiency, individuals with handicaps, and other special populations that traditionally have been underserved in programs for gifted and talented students.

University of Connecticut
2131 Hillside Road, U-7
Storrs, CT 06269-3007
Phone: (806) 486-2900
Website: www.ucc.uconn.edu
E-mail: epsadm06@uconnvm.
     uconn.edu